WHEN A MAN LOVES

WHEN A MAN LOVES

A Lifestyle & Leadership Most
Men Will Never Experience

PETE A. KENNEDY

Copyright © 2020 Pete A. Kennedy
All rights reserved. No part of this book may be used or reproduced in any manner whatsoever without prior written consent of the authors, except as provided by United States of America copyright law.

Published by Best Seller Publishing®, Pasadena, CA
Best Seller Publishing® is a registered trademark
Printed in the United States of America.
ISBN *9798574509272*

This publication is designed to provide accurate and authoritative information with regard to the subject matter covered. It is sold with the understanding that the publisher is not engaged in rendering legal, accounting, or other professional advice. If legal advice or other expert assistance is required, the services of a competent professional should be sought. The opinions expressed by the authors in this book are not endorsed by Best Seller Publishing® and are the sole responsibility of the author rendering the opinion.

For more information, please write:
Best Seller Publishing®
253 N. San Gabriel Blvd, Unit B
Pasadena, CA 91107
or call 1(626) 765 9750
Visit us online at: www.BestSellerPublishing.org

Contents

Introduction 1

Chapter 1: Concrete Jungle 11

Chapter 2: Daddy and Me 25

Chapter 3: Gone Abroad 39

Chapter 4: Losing Daddy, Gaining Brothers 51

Chapter 5: Approaching the Honeycomb 65

Chapter 6: The Secret Sauce to Life, Forgiveness... 79

Chapter 7: Team Together, Team Apart 93

Chapter 8: Strengthening the Arm 105

Chapter 9: Sharing Renewal 117

Conclusion 133

Introduction

Goodwin Park Road

Soap, soap, soap. Come get your soap.

That was the Mr. Soapy song I would hear every Saturday morning as early as 7 o' clock in the morning. Mr. Soapy would come by to sell his soap to our tenement yard since Saturdays were considered a washday for us. Washday was scheduled within the yard due to limited space on the clothesline. My mother was scheduled to wash on Saturdays because she worked during the week. We lived on Goodwin Park Rd. off South Camp Road in Kingston, Jamaica. Our tenement yard was a strip of rooms attached together surrounded by dirt, with an outside bathroom shared by everyone. There was also an outside kitchen, which you could build, and my parents did.

    All us kids in the yard always looked forward to the weekends. After the wake-up call from Soapy, my mother, Mrs. Joyce, would prepare breakfast. Cornmeal porridge with bread or sometimes boiled dumplings with saltfish and callaloo, also known as collard greens. While eating breakfast, sometimes I would hear our neighbors bickering over some issues within the yard. This often happens when you live in a tenement yard in Jamaica; you hear everyone's business. Right after breakfast, I would hear another song yell. This time it was from the ice cream man.

Ice Cream, Ice Cream, A Me Have Di Ice Cream.

It wasn't a truck like in the States. This man rode a bike with an ice crate or bucket tied to the back where he stored his ice cream for sale. Every parent saved some money for Saturday morning to buy their child ice cream. Once we were finished, we would begin to play.

Kingston was in constant hustle and bustle. We didn't live far from the main road called South Camp Road. It was located directly across from the Alpha Boys Academy School. I would feel our walls shake from the neighbor's speakers as they loudly played music on those early Saturday morning.

They would compete with the engines of the city buses as they went by, and bus conductors were yelling, "Downtown! Crossroads!"

They would try to persuade citizens to choose their vehicle as a means of transportation to their destination. The drivers would compete with each other to see who had more passengers at the end of the day.

It was rough living in the inner cities of Kingston. Whenever communities were at war, I would hear sounds of gunfire in the nighttime. More often than not, these fights were violent with a lot of robberies. Once as a child, I found a bullet shell in my yard. Whenever the community was at war, there would be a curfew. Citizens knew when it was time to go inside. This was not an announced curfew by the government; it was a community-known curfew organized by our neighbors.

As a child, my role models were the males who hung out on the street corners. The majority of them, their role model was the politician. These men on the street corner had multiple women and children. Politicians would come to visit our community to form relationships with these males for protection and votes. Imagine the street corner in Jamaica like a mixed salad. It was combined with good, hardworking men, and men affiliated with the gang.

I had very little television to watch because we only had one TV station. Homes did not get telephones until the late 1990s. Communication and exposure were limited to our community unless you traveled outside. So, everything I learned was through my eyes, and what I heard on the street corner. As a boy in Jamaica, I learned that in order to be a man, you needed to have multiple women. These women would become the mothers of our children. The rest of the talk was either about music or violence. The only positive leadership I witnessed at that age was that of my mother. It was the norm for women to become leaders within their homes back then.

My parents were considered a cool couple, Mrs. Joyce and Mr. Ken. They troubled no one. My mother was a Christian who was highly respected in the community. My dad was not a Christian, but he was easygoing. My mother displayed love to everyone, regardless of where you were from or accomplishments. There was no judgment in her eyes. Because of this, everyone looked out for Mrs. Joyce. That respect covered my brother and me. Once she showed love to a young man in our community who had no food and she fed him for a month.

One morning I woke up to a commotion outside. A neighbor frantically woke our family with news that someone was trying to steal a tire from my dad's Hillman Hunter car. The men in the community caught him and wanted the Kennedy family to tell them what to do with this thief. They yelled for Mrs. Joyce. Now, the options were to kill him, beat him badly, or wait until the police arrived. The police could be hours. Back in the 1980s, the police were slow when it came to the inner-city issues of Jamaica. My mother was vocal and displayed her love through consistently seeking peace amongst everyone.

Before my mother could respond, a neighbor shouted, "Mrs. Joyce yuh too nice. Yuh gonna wanna save him for Jesus, we gwan beat him til the police cum." Then the members of the community started to beat this man with bats, boards, and anything they could find. Some threw stones at him until the police came and arrested him. I remember the man bleeding from his head, and his clothes were soaked with blood. The community saved my dad's tire. It struck me years later my dad had no response when he was told someone tried to steal his tires. The community sought leadership direction and decisions from my mother.

It was one of the first times I recall observing leadership displayed by my mother. My dad did and said nothing. As the community called out and asked for my mother's direction, my dad was inside the house for all of it. I learned all my positive leadership from my mother, opposed to the negative one I learned from my dad and the street corner.

Second to my mother was another positive role model in my life. Still to this day, my big brother Marlon has always been there for me. He was tall and slender and lived at home with us. He resembled and behaved like my mother, while I resembled and behaved like my dad. Marlon and I did things differently, but he loved me so much as a brother. His leadership to guide me was phenomenal as we grew up. Marlon would lead by ensuring I was being obedient to our parents. He led with love, always communicating at the highest level. He knew and kept me informed as a younger brother. Most importantly, he led by example. Everything he asked of me, he also did. There were times he would act it first, and then shared a story of how it could be done. I remember when it was getting close to exam time, he would constantly remind me of ways on how to study in order to pass the exam. These were tactics that worked for him when he sat the similar exam few years prior. This was leadership without us knowing. Imagine, if we only had help to develop these behaviors of ours from an early age.

I wouldn't realize until years later what Marlon was doing. He was showing me the leadership I needed, whether or not I recognized it. I believe this strongly as I conducted my search and observation of other leaders. It's best to start early, which is why parents are so critical to the process.

At a John Maxwell International Conference, Dr. Bruce Lipton was scheduled as one of our guest speakers. He was a short guy with a unique voice. He spoke softly and clearly. He wore glasses and had grey hair. This was the first time I had ever seen him speak, and as a speaker myself, I was intrigued. He shared with us that the first seven years of a child's life is critical. This is where they develop all their learning, especially communication skills. For me, those years were at Goodwin Park Road. Dr. Lipton then said something profound that has stuck with me ever since.

He said, "Give me a child for the first seven years, and I'll give you a man or a woman."

I was grateful my father lived at home with us. I had the presence of a man in my home as a visual representation of leadership. He wasn't physically absent. But true leadership comes through influence and leading by example, which was missing from my dad. Leadership for me at that time was my mother and my brother Marlon. I consistently witnessed their behaviors of leadership.

Having children of my own, I now see the impact on a child during the first seven years of their lives. I can say it is worth the investment to set up our youths for success later in life. Some of this investment may require us as parents to invest in ourselves in order to support the child as much as possible. One of the leadership qualities of a leader is to lead by example.

Proverbs 22:6 says, "Train up a child in the way he should go, even when he is old, he will not depart from it."

I encourage you to plan and invest in your children from an early age. In turn, this will have a positive impact in the future.

I also have three older sisters from the same father: Marcia Marie Kennedy was the first, Olivine Veleta Kennedy the second, and Nicolette Natalie Kennedy, the third. They were always visiting on weekends and holidays. Marcia and Olivine would spend days at the house with us because my mother made our home open for everyone, especially families. But from a naming pattern perspective, it seems my dad started the (M.A.K.) Marlon Andrew Kennedy and (P.A.K.) Pete Andre Kennedy idea with my brother and me. My dad's full name was Noel Augustus Kennedy (N.A.K.). We all got along well as siblings.

I am a leadership expert who has been studying and observing leadership attributes and personal behavior profiles for the last 15 years. I have worked in the customer service, banking, and aviation industry as a leader holding positions such as Training Assistant, Trainer, Supervisor, Manager, and Lead Trainer. I have always strived to achieve the desired results per employer. My philosophy on P.I.E. This means performance, image, and exposure, which has rewarded me with many noticeable awards from nominations, top performers, and promotions. Some of these awards are PEAK award winner, Top Trainer, Top Supervisor, just to name a few. I am married to my childhood girlfriend Jillian, and we share two boys, Dontae and Jace. As a leadership expert, I work with small and large organizations, youths, and adults in the areas of personal and professional development for growth in all areas of their life. I teach, train, coach, and speak for organizations, groups, and individuals.

When invited to train, coach, or speak, my audience's age can range from teenagers to elders within our community. My message and workshops are tailored directly to the needs of my clients. These events are based on their goals, whether it is one-on-one coaching or a workshop. Regardless of what I do, there's one message that is used in our business model and that is, "Leadership is Love, Love is Leadership."

I also reflect on my friend John Maxwell's quote 'Leadership is influence, nothing more, nothing less.' As a leader, I serve those I lead by connecting and sharing relatable experiences that can support other leaders. With researched facts and information to guide those, I lead in accomplishing their passion. I am also a servant in the community and consistently volunteering my time to give back. I'm always collaborating with several foundations and offering my services to the community in various ways.

In my professional career, I had the opportunity to travel to all time zones within the United States and internationally. This was to teach, train, coach, and speak to many different age groups and corporations. The intent behind this book is to share with leaders and parents the process or strategy to become successful as a person, leader, and parent by reading my experiences first-hand, which have a proven track record. I also want to encourage these individuals to make sound decisions early and to be there as support, especially to youth needing guidance.

For my Jamaican men, I want to encourage you to stop having your resources tied up in multiple places. This can later set back your success, set you up for failure, or derail the discovery of your passion. My experience and guidance will set you up for success in life, personally and professionally.

This book is broken down into two sections for an easy read and to follow the story.

Roadmap

Part A: Our surroundings
- How our childhood is the foundation of our lives
- How our environment affects our values
- The importance of support and accountability

Part B: Creating a new life
- Forgiveness
- Establishing our MUST-SHOULD-COULD
- Spreading the change we seek to create
- Finding our strengths and weaknesses

I will share the components of the MUST-SHOULD-COULD methodology. This methodology has been a huge success in my life, personally and professionally. All my clients have seen similar success and productive results using this methodology. I expand on each of these through the chapters.

♦ ♦ ♦

Mommy would stop and talk to everyone on her way home. I would watch her as she would inquire about our neighbor's day. Everyone loved her intentional attention. She cared enough to stop and talk to them when she had a family at home waiting. My mother would always look for a win-win resolution out of every situation. She was a woman of peace and disliked conflict. I grew up sharing a lot, as my mother was a role model in the community. Her influence motivated her to continue her education. She worked hard to relocate her talents to a new job. This later afforded her and my dad the purchase of a home in the community next door called Allman Town. We moved into the Arnold Road apartment, and I was happy. No more sharing and using the bathroom outside. My brother and I even got our own room, no more sleeping in the living room. We were no more in a tenement yard and moved into an apartment on the second floor. We had our kitchen and running water. I was happy.

Sadly our island was struck by Hurricane Gilbert two years later. It did not impact my home directly, but the island was destroyed badly. My community was badly impacted. Poverty, crime, and violence were high within our community, but I can truly say I do not know what it means to go to bed hungry and not having clothes, food, or shelter. My parents worked hard to ensure they provided a decent life for my brother and me. This was to protect us from the street corner or gang life.

I believe Jamaica's music, society, culture, and men do not set up youth for success. It was good ole dancehall music. I would always sneak out of the house to attend parties and especially whenever the big sound came into town, like Stone Love. Without effective leadership in a youth's life, music and society will become their lifestyle. This will produce similar unsuccessful results – resorting to violence, or some sort of hustle. The men on the street corners would tell me their survival stories in my community. I do not regret anything in my life; I just wish I had effective leadership, guidance, and support earlier in my life. That is why I wrote this book as well as fulfilling my mission to serve.

My desire for you is not to cope in life but to excel at the highest level. You should strive to live a fulfilled life personally and professionally. Throughout my story, you will learn how effective leadership from an early age can have a tremendous impact on your life. As a parent, this book will show you how you can accomplish this for your children and yourself. As a leader, you can start influencing others earlier for a greater impact. If you are a youth, young adult, or single, how can one lead with love and be effective in doing so?

Chapter 1

Concrete Jungle

(Arnold Road)

Two years after Hurricane Gilbert, we were finally settled at Arnold Road. The island had cleaned up and recovered to the best of its ability, and everyday life was back to normal. I was attending Mico Practicing All-Age school and passed my common entrance exams to enter high school. I was anxious but also excited as we awaited the results from the exam. I was looking forward to high school because I saw it as an opportunity to step out on my own. Marlon was attending Kingston College (KC) high school, which was walking distance from our home. I wanted to be on my own and not follow my brother, so I selected the rival school of choice to attend.

In those days, before taking the high school exam, a child would select two schools of their choice. Based on their exam scores, they would be granted entrance to them or not. My schools of choice were first, Jamaica College (JC) and the second choice was Kingston College (KC). The scores were posted in the newspaper, and I could not wait for mommy to get home with the paper. I knew her schedule and waited downstairs by the gate for her timely 5:45 pm arrival home.

When I saw her coming down the street, I ran to meet her and took the newspaper searching for my name. "Yes!" I shouted and jumped for joy as I saw my name in the newspaper passing the exam for my first school of choice, JC. I was looking forward to the rival trash-talking since my school and Marlon's schools compete in activities throughout the school year. But, the trash-talking began before I even started high school.

I was ready for high school dressed in my sky-blue shirt and navy-blue pants. I was entering the unknown, just happy to start my own thing. Every morning I would walk to the bus for school, while my brother walked to school every morning. During my first year at JC, I represented the school in the "Pepsi Under-13 Boys Soccer Competition." It felt good playing soccer at a competitive level for the first time.

I spent a lot of time at Hope Gardens, a park with roller coaster rides and the like, because that was where the girls who skipped school would hang out also. And now having a little popularity due to soccer it was considered the cool thing to just hang out at the park. Spending so much time at the park, I was reported as absent from class. This resulted in me spending a lot of time at the Vice Principal's office as well as for misconduct behavior in class. The school imported many boys from inner-city neighborhoods to participate in sports. Still, the behaviors came with those boys as well. These boys would stab the conductors on the minibuses on the way home, rob people on the streets in their uniforms, but they did not care. So, my mother decided to transfer me to KC for my second year of high school.

Angry and frustrated, I recalled her words were, "You are not going to Hope Road anymore." Hope Road was the name of the street on which JC was located.

Then she enrolled me at KC, the Melbourne campus.

I believe this was one of the greatest decisions my mother made for me. Most of my friends from the community attended KC at that time. We were a tribe walking to and from school every day. Kizran Levy (Kizzy), my best friend, who was always joking and had a nickname 'Shut' because he would wear this one shirt to school. He would start and stop at my house. We would then be joined by Green a few minutes later, who lived on the back road of my apartment. On our way, we would stop and pick up the two Sawyer brothers and James. If Gary and Clive decided to join us, then we had a total of nine young boys from all different ages walking to and from school.

There was a shortcut on our way to school, which required us to climb over a wall. This was the wall of Sabina Park, where international cricket is played in Jamaica, and it was very tall. The cricket park was connected to a small yard, which had a shorter wall. We would use it to get over the higher wall. That meant we had to climb two walls to get into the park for the shorter route to school.

It was fun some mornings because Gary was a big guy and weighed a lot. It was difficult for him to get over the wall and sometimes needed help. We would laugh and make fun of him. It would require Gary to stand on someone's hand to climb onto the wall and someone had to hold his book bag in the meantime. But he would get us back by saying he would not assist us with our homework later since Gary was the smart guy in the group. On the mornings where we were early for school, we would take the long route to avoid Gary from climbing over the fence.

After school and on weekends, we would play soccer in front of my house on the small two-lane concrete road. We would place bricks as our goals and would move out the way for cars whenever they were passing. They said I was the loudest and the youngest and always seem to get my way. This is where my mother's loving nickname for me was born: she called me Stumps. Later, everyone called me 'Stumpy'. This was for the same reason they called me daddy when I played soccer. I was the youngest and smallest but could be heard the most. Whenever we played, I would be chosen to select the teams. Even though sometimes my friends disagreed with my selection, they went along with my decision. This was leadership and influence from an early age.

Attending KC were my glory years. I learned so much. Mostly because of my coach, Mr. Stratton Palmer. He saw leadership qualities in me and exposed me to leadership. I represented KC in soccer in the Colts '93 & '94 season. Coach Palmer was short in stature and had a bald head. He was also a past student of KC who was now the coach of the under-14 soccer team. He always led by example. He played with us boys as we practiced on numerous occasions, in his dress shoes and attire from work, showing us how to pass the ball from one end of the field to the other. He was always punctual and visible; I cannot recall him missing a practice or game both seasons he was the coach. I respected him the most for how he communicated. He treated us with respect and spoke to us as intelligent and smart young adult men.

I remember once he challenged me to stick to the process and play at a higher level. But after those two seasons, there was no further leadership from a male perspective because my brother had enrolled in the Jamaican military as an officer and began to travel. This allowed my attention to wander elsewhere. Being popular and having a girlfriend became my focus. I played one season of Manning Cup, then graduated from high school. I left high school with a certificate and a few CXC subjects but never crossed the stage as a graduate, all because of bad behavior throughout our entire final year of high school. Boys from that senior year missed a lot of classroom time, involved in gang-related activity, which was brought onto the school campus. And fighting in the school chapel, just to name a few. Oh, I yearned for the feeling of crossing a stage as a graduate. I witnessed Marlon when he graduated, and I wanted to experience the same for myself.

While I played soccer Kizzy and I became close friends because he played soccer also. As a matter a fact he introduced me and supported me in playing the game. He was a year older than me, which made us eligible to play on the same teams together. We played games together, practiced together, as well as played the same position on the field. Other than walking to school with schoolmates, there were a few other boys who were a part of our crew, either as relative or neighbor. O'Neil 'Bang Bell', Kizzy's older brother, Oden 'Hamma', Kizzy's younger brother. Karl 'Aids' my neighbor, Goods from Water Street and Darney. These boys made up our crew. Soccer helped Kizzy and I become closer than everyone else. He was a little taller than me and bigger in structure.

I remember once Kizzy and I were walking home from soccer practice, and we decided to take a shortcut. We were tired and wanted to get home faster. We decided to walk through a gully, located behind St. George's high school to get home. During our walk, we heard the sound of dogs racing towards us, but they were not barking. Kizzy shouted, "Stumpy, run." With our soccer shoes in our hands, we took off running. We didn't want to be caught, attacked, and bitten by these dogs. We got to the side of the gully where we needed to cross over to get to the other side. Every other time we got to this point, it took some time for me because I was afraid of falling into the gully. I would get on my knees and crawl. The citizens of the community had placed a log as a mini bridge to allow for the commute back and forth.

As we approached the bridge, with the dogs closing in on our gap, Kizzy knew that the dogs would stop at the bridge and yelled, "Stumpy, you go pon di bridge first."

When we got to the bridge, Kizzy helped me cross the bridge standing up and quickly. We made it across safely without the dogs catching us. This was love, but as boys raised in a culture, we're taught not to express love with words or physical touch. We did not share it verbally but would die for each other.

Amongst our crew, there was only one father present: my father. He would stay in the house, but we knew he was there. Because of my dad's lack of visibility, we nicknamed him 'not the mama' from the cartoon called Dinosaurs. We did this because we felt he was not fit to be called dad. So, as boys, we listened to the men on the street corners as they would aggressively and violently discuss certain topics and try to express themselves.

From the age of 15 through 17 years old, leadership was nonexistent in my life. Kizzy and I tried to figure out stuff for ourselves. I remember dancehall artist Beenie Man had a song which became my lifestyle entitled 'Nuff Gyal'. I could relate to this song, as Beenie Man named neighboring communities like 'Jungle' and 'Rema', which I was familiar with living in Allman Town. The lyrics go like this 'So Man fi have nuff gal, an gal inna bundle Gal From Rema, gal from Jungle Nuff Gal an none a dem musn't grumble, All ghetto youth unno fi tek mi example". Man, did I love this song, and what an impact it had on my life.

When I heard this song, I felt like one of the men on the street corner because I had multiple girlfriends and was playing soccer. I had two girlfriends at the time, Marie and Simone. Marie was from southside Kingston, and Simone was from my community. I tried to separate them to avoid any conflicts or problems. This was how my habit of having multiple girlfriends started. None of my friends would correct me because it was the norm. Even my brother couldn't say anything. It was the lifestyle of a Jamaican man.

Based on my experience, I do not think my Jamaican society sets up our youth for success. The Beenie Man song was embedded in the subconscious mind, and it became my reality. I could speak to my multiple girlfriends in any manner, even lying. As a young boy growing up, I never heard the word love mentioned. It had a negative connotation within the community. The one place I found love in a positive connotation was in church. When I attended church, we would read about love in the Bible or hearing my mother say, 'I love you, son.' In our community, a man who expressed love was considered weak or homosexual, even if he was straight and said it to his female partner. And in Allman Town, you do not want to be considered as a gay man because the community would gang up and beat you.

I was craving a role model, and like any son, I was seeking it from my father. I wanted to be around my dad so much. When I was not in his presence (which was often), I would emulate him by wearing his outfits. I adored how he dressed; he was a man well put together. All his shirts were ironed before worn; he had some that were worn only on a special occasion, like to a party or a dinner he was invited to. He had some great smelling cologne that got me attention every time I wore it. He eventually discovered I was wearing it because the bottle would deplete faster.

One of the places I would emulate my dad was at the street dances when Stone Love, the number one DJ sound system in Jamaica, would come into town. Kizzy and I would plan our outfit, and I would start hiding my dad's shirt. This was so he did not wear it before the dance. It was the place to be, and I had to look cool! The night of the party, I waited until my mother fell asleep, then snuck out the house through the back door. When I got dressed, my dad's shirt hung almost like a dress on me. The neck button of the shirt was down to my chest. But that was the style back then: baggy shirt and jeans. I would slip on his gold bracelet that was so big that I had to spread my fingers wide, so it would not fall off my wrist because it was too big. But it was worth the risk because it was gold. None of my friends had one, and I thought it would attract girls. I wanted to represent the Kennedy household at any cost at that age.

♦ ♦ ♦

Be Not Conformed

There is a section in the bible that says, "Do not be conformed to this world, but be transformed by the renewal of your mind."

We may have been raised in a concrete jungle environment, but it does not mean we have to conform to the ways and values of its lifestyle. It is hard as a parent who is raising children in a concrete jungle because they cannot escape the outside influences. The meaning of a concrete jungle is a modern city or urban area, especially when perceived as an unpleasant or challenging place to live.

Parenting is not easy:

(1) it was not created for single parenting
(2) parenting is the biggest decision to step into leadership, which a lot of parents do not realize.

The most crucial part of parenting is leading by example. I saw this leadership trait in my soccer coach and my brother, but not in my dad. In the concrete jungle, we need more leaders to lead by example. This behavior will help to change the mindset of our youth and equip them mentally to help them make sound decisions towards their future.

Dr. Bruce Lipton says, give me a child and I give you in return a man or a woman. I heard him say this at the John Maxwell International conference held twice a year in Orlando, FL. He is a stem cell biologist, and bestselling author of 'The Biology of Belief'. He was soft-spoken but spoke clearly for all to understand him. I learned from Dr. Lipton's years of study that the first seven years of a child's life are the most critical. He states these years can make or break a person based on how they are programmed. I believed in his study since I was a past youth director and worked with children from different backgrounds. I noticed that the parents who invest the time and effort to ensure their children are well prepared for the world's responsibilities had more success than those who invested very little. Some of these investments involve being a leader, leading by example, communicating, being trustworthy, and honest. This process will set up youth for success.

Behaviors are developed from lifestyle provisions like role models, creating vision boards, and purposeful commitments. It is by implementing integrity and standards with support or accountability. But how can one advance when the concrete jungle is surrounding you? I recommend identifying positive role models within your community. If these do not exist, look outside your community but choose a person you connect with and who can relate to your struggle.

When Marlon was about to graduate from high school, I recall him writing down on index cards the plans for his life. He had plan A, to be a professional cricket player, or plan B, to become an officer in the military. Plan B worked out for him. Kizzy and I used to make fun of him when we were younger because we have never heard anyone on the street corner mention this approach. We thought it was weird, and he would say, "You gwan laugh at me, yuh a idiot."

All this time my brother was taking the right approach living in the concrete jungle but not having the mindset of the concrete jungle. Marlon was never on the street corners listening to those men, which made a difference in character between us.

Evaluate, Connect, & Renew Your Mind

Why is it some people survive and uplift themselves from such a place? It starts with knowing who you are. As parents, we play a huge role in helping our children identify themselves, supporting them in enhancing their characters, and holding them accountable. Now, the bottleneck in this approach is that we as parents do not know who we are; therefore, how to support our children in this manner.

There are four behavior styles that exist: 1. Thinker, 2. Entertainer, 3. Controller, and 4. Feeler. These styles are mentioned in the DISC behavior profile as Dominance, Influence, Steadiness & Conscientiousness, which you learn from a coach. We are predominantly one of these behaviors but can flex and act in any of the four depending on the situation and also who we are interacting with. Identifying, accepting, and operating in this style is the first place to start. This will allow you to identify other behaviors and help you understand how to interact and enhance those relationships. By doing this, a parent can support a child in doing the same thing, identifying, accepting, and operating in their behavior style while knowing how to interact with others.

There is still hope if you are that parent, individual, or youth. What you need to do is register for any workshop which offers self-identification and implementation of this behavior. Many of us already have an idea of this behavior but need support in applying it. Others need to identify the behavior as well as work on the implementation. If you are still living in the concrete jungle, one of the easiest ways to identify what your current journey looks like is to ask yourself, "am I doing anything different than those around me?" If not, then your results may be similar to what traditionally comes out of the concrete jungle.

This is the time to start making changes. Parents, children learn from what they see, so your words weigh very little in comparison to your actions. Lead by example, seek role models and accountability partners. Once you have identified your behavior style/profile, start mastering the behavior and own it. People will respect it; relationships and goals will become easier to manage and attain. I wish I had someone to help me identify these behaviors from an early age. I would have saved a lot of relationships and helped enhance the life path of many.

As a child, I was not aware of the political party my parents supported, which they kept secret because gangs would become violent around election time. They would harass people into voting for their candidate. Rather than communicating, my parents remained quiet. This had a great impact on me and is where a lot of Jamaican parents go wrong. We scream at our children to not talk to us when we are talking to them. Communication is a two-way format to express oneself and connect with others. Mrs. Joyce had raised us in the church, and we went every Sunday. I had been an active member of youth fellowship and attended youth camps and church trips. Because of this, I was not new to the Bible and its stories; they had now become a part of my lifestyle.

In Jamaica, our parents tell us not to speak. This is a reason men from my island cannot communicate well. When we do, we are considered different and weak. Allow your children to speak and share. Listen to what they are saying. Great leaders listen well. Many times what the child has to say makes sense. They are saying the same thing we are saying as parents. We just fail to see it because it is not how we want them to communicate.

♦ ♦ ♦

In 1994, we won the Colts finals against Norman Manley. We had lost to them in the finals the prior year. It was the first time I had accomplished something as a leader which brought some exposure in our community and school, which earned us huge respect. It was rough in our neighborhood. Although we were respected, I remember one tournament, Kizzy and I played four back-to-back final games. The gunmen were about our age. They lived in our community and sometimes hung out on the street corner with us. They decided we were not going to win, and we had to be beaten. No one could beat us. They were not going to hurt us but refused to hand over our reward, and every game we played we won. They finally gave up but only gave us a box a Guinness, which we could not drink by ourselves, so we shared it. And they kept the money. I recall we still felt like winners of it all because the entire community spoke about it, which was more embarrassing. This exposure allowed Kizzy and I to lay our hands on a gun called the 'one pop'. It was a gun made of board, iron, and spring and can only fire one bullet at a time. No one knew we had it because Kizzy and I kept it as our secret. Along with the gun came women. Kizzy and I both had multiple girlfriends. We dated Marie and Sharon who were sisters and lived in Tivoli Gardens. Along with Marie, I dated Simone, while Kizzy dated Nadine, who were both from Allman Town, our community. Months later, we met Carol and Denise, who were sisters, and added them to the list of other girlfriends we dated. At this time, we were dating three girls each. Looking back I am not sure how we managed not being caught. But in Jamaica this is the norm, it is what we have heard and witnessed on the street corners where the men spoke. Wearing my dad's clothes and jewelry, playing club and high school soccer, having girlfriends, and a gun, I thought we had hit the lottery.

Living in the city of Kingston, my home was the place to stay whenever family members would come into the city for business. My grandmother was living in Chicago and filed for her children and grandchildren to live in America. Several of my family members filed and moved to Chicago to join my grandmother. She wanted to give us all an opportunity for a better life. All my aunts, uncles, and cousins were at the house preparing to emigrate. It was fun having everyone at the house. I had to give up my bed, which was the norm whenever we had a guest. We played family games like dominoes, ludi, and cooked food daily until it was time for them to emigrate.

I felt sad as the fun ended, and I was going to miss my family. We are close. My mother was the only sibling amongst her family who was married, which is why our family did not migrate with everyone when they left. We had to wait a while longer for the approval of our filing. Once my family members left, I was right back to the concrete jungle life.

ACTIVITY

Write down your standards and recite them to memorize them. This way they become a part of your subconscious mind.

_____
_____
_____
_____
_____
_____
_____
_____
_____
_____
_____
_____
_____
_____
_____
_____
_____
_____
_____
_____
_____
_____
_____

Chapter 2

Daddy and Me
(Role Models, Practice, and Connection)

As early as I can recall in high school, I wanted to be around my dad all the time. He was friendly, and everyone seemed to like him. He spoke to everyone, no matter who you were. He was always well-groomed and wore mostly polo t-shirts or a button-down shirt. He was a stocky guy about 5ft 11in tall who wore glasses and would tuck his shirt in his pants as a part of his attire. He was known for wearing some of the cleanest and latest footwear.

He was always on the go and provided for our family financially in the best way he could. He visited the countryside a lot and always promised to take me. But I only remember going once. I kept waiting and believing he would someday take me. It happened so much that my mother nicknamed him 'Promise'. My dad's inability to keep his word made it essential for me to keep mine.

But when the chance to hang out with him arose, I took it, even if it was just to the grocery store. On Fridays, he would take me grocery shopping, as we made small talk and roamed through the aisles. I would watch him as he grabbed four loaves of bread. But later that evening, I would only see one loaf in the cupboard. As a child growing up in Jamaica, you are taught not to ask questions, so I did not ask where the other loaves of bread were going. Man, did I yearn for my dad's love!

When I lost my virginity at the age of 12, I wish my dad had been there to provide some guidance. One day he caught me having sex with Denise, one of my girlfriends, and said, "I am going to tell your mother when she gets home," and stormed out my room.

But he never said a word. I think because, internally, he liked that his son was having sex with a girl. I can imagine he may have bragged to his friends about it. My dad had no idea when I needed his support. This was solely because we had very little interaction, so he had no idea when something was wrong.

By my senior year in high school, neither of my parents had seen me play soccer. My mother could not attend the games because she had to work and cook dinner when she got home. We would talk about the game when I got home because she had listened to the radio. It felt good talking to mommy about my games because she was my only emotional support in the house at that time. Marlon was still away in the military. Inner-city parents did not support their children because of either work or taking care of the household and younger siblings.

◆ ◆ ◆

It was Manning Cup season. The Manning Cup is the highest level of schoolboy soccer in Jamaica. KC was playing against Wolmer's Boys high school. My next-door neighbor 'Aids' attended Wolmer's Boys, so the trash-talking began. We talked about whose team was better and had better players. At that time Wolmer's had a talented player called 'Bibi' Gardner, who later represented the island in the soccer World Cup tournament.

Trash-talking was one of my strengths, and I took it to the field. I would try to intimidate my opponent by whispering silly things in their ears when I stood next to them on the field. One game I told the opponent, "His knees were so big, I am not sure if he was in the right game." He was so confused. He said, "What do you mean?". At this time, had distracted him mentally from the game as I began to get into his head. Other times, I would shout at them every time I stole the ball. I would remind them of how weak and lacking as a player they were. This put my team in a better position to win.

Days leading up to the game, we argued whose team was better on street corners. The community was excited as we got prepared to compete. Every time Kizzy and I walked the streets people would yell at us, "Mmek sure yuh win di game eno."

Some would ask if we needed anything. It was one of the first times I can remember being loved outwardly by other men in the community, which at that time felt weird. I felt the love once when an elderly man from the community tried to command me to go home because it was getting late, and he wanted to ensure I got enough rest for the game. They wanted us to win!

It was game day, and we were the home team. The entire Allman community came to cheer on Kizzy and me. The game had started, and the score was 0-0. Coach Bell was the coach of the Manning Cup team.

"Stumpy," he called, and I jumped up off the bench.

Elated and nervous at the same time, the four sides of the field were packed with spectators. People were cheering and chanting, drums playing, and KC boys were singing. Coach Bell said 'warm'; that meant get ready. I ran up and down the side of the field getting ready to enter the game.

The coach called again, "Stumpy, come here."

Then he shared with me the game plan. This time, it was different than what we practiced. He said, "I am putting you in at left midfield." This was new for me because my normal position was a defender. Already nervous but elated; this was not a position I practiced.

I said, "Coach, left mid."

He said, "Just run!"

The game paused on an out ball, and the referee blew the whistle for my entrance. A few minutes into the game, one of my teammates passed a through ball, and I took off running. Zoom! I was quick and got to the ball before the opponent. I realized it was just me and the goalkeeper. Boom! Off the left foot, I took a shot towards goal, but this was my weaker shooting leg. The ball went to the opposite side of the field. But an oncoming teammate tapped the ball in the goal. KC scored and was up 1-0.

The crowd started to cheer, and spectators ran onto the field. They lifted me onto their shoulders and shouted," Goal! Goal! Goal!"

I was happy that I was able to assist my team in scoring. Since I am normally defense, I am not used to being a part of scoring the goals. This is what it felt like to be a scorer.

As I was being lifted onto the shoulders of parents and community members, my dad was sitting in his usual rum bar. As he sipped his Jamaican white rum on the rocks, Mr. Mack, the bartender, was listening to the game on the shop radio. Mr. Mack started to cheer in the bar when he heard of the goal, and my name was mentioned with the assist. Even then with my dad's name 'Kennedy' mentioned on the radio, he missed it.

Mr. Mack ran up to my father and said, "Ken, yuh nuh hear yuh bwoy name pon di radio, KC score!"

Feeling proud, excited, and guilty all in one, my dad left the bar. He wanted to show his love in the only way he knew how.

He went to downtown Kingston and purchased a pair of soccer shoes for me. When he got home, I was already home. He came into the room and handed me the box. He said here, try these. I was excited to see what my dad had bought me. I began to open the box. To my surprise, inside the box, was a pair of soccer shoes, a style I had never seen before. The normal soccer shoes have 12 studs underneath and these had 34 studs and they were not the turf style.

I sadly looked at the shoes and said, "Daddy, I cannot bring these to school."

I then removed a pair of soccer shoes from underneath my bed and showed him in comparison.

I said, "Daddy, I will get laughed at school for wearing these shoes."

I had a pair of Adidas Copa Beckenbauer. These were worn in the International World Cup at the time. I placed the gift under my bed and never wore them.

My dad saw this. Due to his basic education, he stepped back rather than stepping up. He left school at an early age and never finished his education. But he worked hard. I believe because of his lack of leadership skills, he missed an opportunity to connect with me. I did not know how to feel since I wanted this relationship with him even though I had the community behind me. But the support a child craves from their parents is undying. Even if they become world-famous, they will always crave the approval of their parents. At this point, I felt I had the support I needed, but it was outside my house.

I was searching for a role model. One would hope that my own father would have filled that position, but I had to seek it elsewhere. It is essential to find strong, guiding role models early in life. But they are not always handed to you.

Role Models (Who leads the team?)

It was difficult to discover good role models as I grew up in the inner city. What I have discovered is that those who have risen above the inner city find themselves moving out of the inner city and moving to the uptown OR to the Portmore area.

Therefore, it is difficult to find good role models within the inner-city communities. I am not recommending anyone to remain in the inner-city if the opportunity presents itself for you to leave, but one must give back. Some may say it is unsafe to go directly back to the neighborhoods they were raised in because of the violence and uncertainty of their protection. No matter where you are from, I recommend to my readers to give back within the schools of those communities. You can donate funds or send supplies. By doing this, you are making an impact within the same community in which you were raised. This follows one of my philosophies: TEAM. Together Each Achieves More. Again, this speaks to leading by example. If we are going to work as a team, there needs to be a leader for someone to follow.

Years later when I moved to Florida, I became a youth director. Our teenage group met weekly on Friday evenings. I noticed in a few sessions our young people, who were predominantly from the inner city, were distracted and consistently on their cell phones. At our first meeting, I shared with them that as their youth director, I was not impressed with their lack of attention during youth fellowship meetings. I wanted to learn why, and how could we incorporate the things that interested them with what we were doing. So, I decided to host a few sessions discussing social media and talk about who they followed online. By knowing who they follow, I know who influences their actions and perceptions of the world.

Our breaking moment came by taking this approach. They began to openly share the content on social media that was keeping them engaged. There was a new application called Facebook. They were able to follow and watch their favorite celebrity or whomever they felt was a person of interest to them. This was the first session when some of our new teenagers actually spoke and interacted with everyone else, so I decided

I needed to continue this topic for more engagement, which could be used for other topics as I got to know more about these youths.

So, we left the first session with the following homework: the youths were to create a list of people who were their role models or celebrities they followed on social media. They were to tell us why they were a person of interest to them and bring their name to the next session. I could not help but think about how much music and celebrities influenced my understanding of my culture and behavior. And at this time, when teens are impenetrable but analyzing, a role model can really make a difference. I wanted to help them question their role models.

Our next session was even more interesting and a huge learning moment. This was the first time I truly realized and experienced different behavior styles and values. The youths were truly expressing themselves based on their beliefs. The only thing I asked them to do was to share and respect each other's views. I managed this carefully. Out of that meeting, relationships grew. As a leader, I grew as well. I understood how powerful personal behaviors are and how impacting our environment is to us as we grow.

I again, support Dr. Bruce Lipton's views on raising children. During our session, I would research the lives of those role models and discuss them with the group. Then we would decide to keep or discard a role model after Googling them. Eighty percent of the role models the youths had were discarded and changed.

Connection is critical to the process and elements of leadership, especially within the family structure. Growing up on the street corners of Allman Town, Jamaica, men predominantly hung out and talked all day long. These men were connecting with each other. Connection is where influence takes place.

Leaders get to lead, and those they lead get to grow. At these street gatherings, stories were shared about life experiences involving mostly women, music, and crime, which derived directly from politics. I have discovered that regardless of whether the conversations were positive or negative, people love to connect. Once they do, they will invest their personal time to whatever they are connected. This is where leaders become vulnerable, but the risk and price are worth it all.

In order to connect, the leader or parent must share a life experience of failure and then success with details of how it was accomplished. Many leaders and parents struggle with this critical step in the process because some consider it as displaying weakness, especially in the Jamaican culture. As I witnessed people connecting wherever I went, I discovered men will talk outside their home but become quiet once inside their home. Therefore, in my culture, men do not connect because it is seen as weak. This in turn impacts our leadership, our opportunity to connect and grow, and as well, enhancing their relationships. How can one avoid this and still connect? A leader needs to write down his stories/experiences and practice them, so when needed they are ready to be delivered.

Practice: Why do I need to write down my stories?

Leaders need to write down their stories the way we update our resumes with our jobs and accomplishments. Practicing this behavior, the leader can identify what and how much of the story they want to share, and what story would fit best based on the issue at hand. Having stories to share as a leader or parent are great ways to connect and influence. This preparation will set up a leader for success when they can share in the moments that they are needed; this also makes them relatable to the other person.

We were all born leaders. But to be an effective leader, one must practice and develop those leadership skills. Just as a professional soccer player practices to become efficient at the game, we must take a similar approach to leadership. If it is not practiced, those skills will not grow. Practice! Practice! Practice!

As a child, we do not get to choose who our leaders are. This is why when one makes the decision to become a parent, one is also making the decision to become a leader. It starts at home. Becoming a parent is an automatic promotion to leadership.

True Leadership (Figuring It Out On My Own)

I remember once hanging with my dad and saw that he was talkative amongst his peers. He was leading, being the main speaker, giving directions, and being asked questions. He hosted a wedding reception once and took me along with him. He was captivating in his words as he spoke to the audience; everyone was engaged as he grabbed their attention with his jokes. Like usual, everyone loved his attire. It was simple but he just had a natural swag; everything he wore was to another level. He was totally comfortable in his fashion. This was the first time I was exposed to public speaking as a child. I wish I had been exposed to more of this man who was always so silent at home. I loved it; this was the leader I wished was at home.

Additionally, my dad had a lot of female friends. That is what he told me they were. Later, I discovered that these were women he was having affairs with. But even with all his cheating behavior, I cannot recall seeing my parents in an argument. If it happened, I was never around to witness it.

Every year, one of my parents would travel to the US while the other parent stayed with us at home. This turn was my mother's; she was visiting my grandmother, aunts, uncles, and cousin. They had left a few years ago and were now residing in Chicago,

IL. One day while mommy was on her trip, dad brought one of his female friends to our home while I was there. Our kitchen faced another neighbor's kitchen. Ms. Brown, my friend Aids' mother, saw my dad's female friend in the house.

In shock and disappointment, Ms. Brown yelled, "Ken a which woman that yuh have inna Joyce house?"

Immediately dad and his female friend left.

I was speechless. I didn't know what was going to happen when mommy returned. I did not know how to feel, whether this was right or wrong. Our culture supported this behavior. This is what the men on the corner spoke about. My brother was also not at home at the time. If Marlon had been at home, my dad wouldn't have brought home that woman. Marlon was older and would have made sense of the situation. Maybe he would have said something to my dad. I felt he knew how much I wanted this father-son relationship and that I would not break the man code. This was not the leadership one should display. I knew that when my mom returned, Ms. Brown was definitely going to share what she witnessed.

When my mom returned home, I was more excited about what she had brought for me and Marlon. I totally forgot the day dad brought another lady to the house and was seen by Ms. Brown. That very same week, I was downstairs and heard a commotion upstairs in our house. My mother was yelling and screaming, "lick mi if yuh bad ken, lick mi."

I quickly ran upstairs to discover my mom had found out what he was doing while she was traveling. This was the first time I had heard my mother speaking loudly in an angry tone of voice. I did not know how to react. My mom confronted dad about his actions. My dad felt that his way out of the situation was to be abusive physically, the normal way for a Jamaican man. The leader within me would not allow me to stand to the side and watch my dad abuse my mother.

So, I stepped in between them and said, "Daddy if yuh lick mommy, we ago war today because you know yuh were wrong."

He was shocked and then turned his attention to me. How dare I stand up to the man of the house!

That day, I committed myself to stand with my mother and let my dad know that I knew what was going on. It would not be tolerated in this house. Even though I felt this way, I was already programmed to the mental abuse and character of a Jamaican young man. We hated informants, but I was not going to allow this abuse to happen to my mother. From an early age, I made the decision I will not abuse or allow abuse to happen to any woman in my presence. Even after that incident, I still had a lot of respect for my dad because of the culture programmed mentally towards women. I should have shared with my mother what had happened while she was away and not let the neighbor do it. But I was committed to the man code. I didn't realize that the man code, in many cases, does not display effective leadership. As a leader, you are never wrong for doing what is right.

Although I can recall spending some quality time with my dad, I learned things from seeing. Since my dad didn't speak to me much, I had to figure out things on my own rather than being led. When it came to his family, he was a man of little words. But amongst his friends, he was seen as a leader.

However, I know now that true leadership starts at home with our loved ones, spouse, partner, children. Our home is our safe place to practice and learn those leadership skills which we can take into the workplace for further development. We were all born leaders but to be an effective leader one has to practice and develop those leadership skills, just as a professional soccer player practices to become efficient at the game. We have to take a similar approach to leadership; if not practiced those skills will not grow.

Activity

Role Models and Lessons

- Three Steps: Outside of their environment, Family/Past, Current.

Step 1: Think of someone outside of your environment that you look up to...

Example:
- Celebrity, Speaker, Author, etc.
- Why would you consider them a role model?
- _____
- What is the impact of that?
- _____
- If you research a little about them online, are you affirmed by anything?
- _____
- Shocked?
- _____
- If shocked, would you still consider them a role model?
- _____
- If affirmed, what do you carry forward from their example?
- _____

Step 2: Now think of someone from your family/past that you looked up to...

- Why were they a role model?
- _____
- What was the impact of that?
- _____

- Is there anything from their life that might negate that for you?
- No, because _____

Or
- Yes, because _____
- Do you still consider them a role model today?
- _____
- If so, how do you carry forward their example?
- _____

Step 3: Who do you look up to today?
- Why are they a role model?
- _____
- What is the impact of that?
- _____
- Is there anything from their life that might negate that for you?
- No, because _____

Or
- Yes, because _____
- How do you hope to carry their example forward?
- _____

Chapter 3

Gone Abroad

(No Change, No Improvement)

Three years later, it was our family's turn to emigrate to Chicago, IL. Marlon was no longer eligible to move with us because he was 21 and was considered an adult. Marlon wanted to see me succeed. I was smoking weed at the time.

One day he said to me, "Pete, this is an opportunity, do not mess it up."

He continued to say, "If I catch you smoking, I am going to tell mommy."

Kizzy and I would hide and smoke to avoid him from catching us. But he knew I was still doing it but was trying to protect me. This was Marlon expressing his love for me.

On an evening flight to Chicago, my mother, my dad, and I left Jamaica on March 31, 1997. I remember sitting on the bench as we waited for the immigration officer to hand us our green card. Yes, back then, you received your green card at the airport. It was my grandmother who filed for her children and grandchildren to move to the US for the opportunity for a better life.

Grandma Mable was a short woman with bowlegs. She had the cleanest ears I have seen. Her ability to somehow hear everything was remarkable. She was a woman of great wisdom. The stories she would share and the direction she gave us always worked. One of the greatest behaviors she taught was to communicate and look in someone's eyes. She said 'Stumps, people eyes will tell you the truth, look at them when you talking to someone.' She had first moved to Canada and then to the US. April 1st, 1997 was my first morning permanently in America. For Americans, this day is normally considered 'All Fool's Day,' which is when they play tricks on each other. Two weeks later, my dad went back home to Jamaica to finish his tenure at his job where he worked for over 25 years. He had just a few more years to retire.

It was a bittersweet moment because I didn't know what to expect. The night before I left, Kizzy and I spent a lot of time sitting on the sidewalk discussing what our experiences might look like. What exciting things I could do like playing soccer in the States. We also talked about remaining close and not letting anyone replace our friendship. When I got the chance, I would visit and try to help him to travel to the States one day as well.

As the days got closer, Kizzy and I kept my travel a secret except for our families, whom we trusted. In Jamaica, whenever anyone from the Ghetto was traveling, it was a kept secret until the day of the travel. They said it was to remain safe before one would travel.

♦ ♦ ♦

Growing up, we did not have phones in our home. In the last quarter of 1996, the entire community had phones installed in their homes. Having a new way to communicate was cool as a teenager, and I would call Kizzy in the morning to talk about our plan for the day. Many times, with nothing to do, we just sat and watched people and vehicles as they went by. When it became nighttime, we would seek the presence of our girlfriends. This is where I was torn at times, wanting to be in the presence of both Kizzy and my girlfriends.

I would have Marie visit me early because she lived in a high crime-infested community, and we did not want her traveling late. Right after Marie would leave, I would visit Denise for a short time, then spend the rest of the night with Simone. Sometimes we would gather as friends and share stories and jokes. This felt good and I felt loved. Love must be taught, and in the Jamaican inner-city communities, expressing this love in a sincere brotherly manner was not accepted. Loyalty was required without expressing such love. Kizzy knew that all we had done together would remain between us. What a way to confuse a child from an early age.

My mother knew I loved playing soccer and knew I wanted to become a professional soccer player. That is the dream of most Jamaican young boys. So, my expectation of school after migrating was one with extracurricular activity like soccer, basketball, etc. My mother made an appointment with a school for us to discuss their options available and whether this school would be a good fit for me. When we arrived at the appointment and entered the school, I started to look for the soccer field, basketball court, or track field. But there were none to be found.

During the interview, the administrator realized I was not mentally in the room and distracted. He asked me what was wrong?

I said to him, "Where is the soccer field or something?"

He explained that this was a technical school, and it did not offer any extracurricular activity like sports. This was DeVry Institute of Technology, now known as DeVry University.

With the shock and disappointment on my face, my mother turned to me and said, "Computers are next to rule the world, and that is what you need to study, son."

The rest was history.

I was in total disagreement with this process. But a Jamaican parent dictates what their children do. This is another bad cultural tradition. Parents should understand their child and guide them to their purpose, not force them to do what they think would work.

♦ ♦ ♦

Little did I know, America would play a trick on me. One month after moving to the States, on my 18th birthday, I was a suspect in a murder case.

The first time I went home with a beeper and a cell phone, my mother said, "Stumps, be careful. We know Chicago neighborhoods are rough with a lot of gangsters and drug selling around. Please stay focused and remember the reason why you are here."

I got a job at a grocery store, Dominick's, pretty quickly after arriving. I remember pushing shopping carts for Dominick's in Evanston. Wintertime was the worst. Pushing 15-20 shopping carts through the snow was difficult.

My cousin Shana had been living in Chicago for some time and dated a drug dealer named Tony. Naturally, I would hang out with my cousins a lot, so Tony and I became close friends. He introduced me to the Gangster Disciple (GD) gang and drug-selling world. My mother and family at this time were totally aware of my lifestyle. So to keep my family safe, I moved out of the house. In comparison to my job pushing carts at Dominick's, I made way much more money selling drugs as a GD. I bought a car, and I quit Dominick's job.

By this time, the gang was where I found my refuge and love. The guys I sold drugs with always looked out for me. They showed they cared by calling to check in, giving me support on the street, and access to cars. But all this love was surrounded by illegal and negative activity. They taught me how to cook my own cocaine, purchase my own gun, and how to remain low under the radar while hustling. As Jamaicans, we were using the gang as our protection but also a guaranteed market for us to sell our drugs since we had access to all the weight (huge amounts of drugs). I was taught how to buy a scale and how to transport it when preparing my drugs for sale. Where was the positive and upright leadership? Nowhere to be found. I was taught when and how to wear my black and red outfit and not be noticed.

Since I made my own money and had a car, I was able to travel wherever I wanted. One night, I was in downtown Evanston at Burger King with some friends. I met Melanie there. A few weeks later, we started dating. Since I was taught to have multiple girlfriends, Melanie was added to the list with Kim. I met Kim through my cousin Annmarie. Kim was quiet and did not leave the house much. Melanie could leave her house at any time she wanted. So, it was easy to keep them apart. Melanie and I became closer as we spent a lot of time on the streets together due to her availability.

After months of going back and forth between my mom's house and my cousin's house, I moved into Melanie's home with her mother, older brother, and younger sister. Her nickname was 'Shorty' because she was short and petite but quick at the mouth. When we met, she told me she was 18. But after moving in, I discovered she was only 16. Her mother allowed us to continue dating. I kept quiet because I had a place to sleep and hustle while attending school. While living with Melanie, I ensured she had everything. I would take her to school every morning and pick her up until I taught her how to drive a manual car. She would brag to her friends whenever she drove to school. The leader within me wanted to see her succeed, so I met all her personal needs, and a year later, she graduated high school.

No matter what, I was committed to two things when I moved to the States; they were as follows:

1. I am not going to jail for any female/woman.
2. I am not getting anyone pregnant. If I do, I am staying, and she's stuck with me. At least, for the next 21 years.

These were my rules while I lived the life of a drug dealer, gangster, and student. No matter how many girlfriends I had, I ensured that I protected myself sexually. I knew I did not want these girls as a wife. The lifestyle of a drug dealer, gangster, and my charisma especially made it easy for me to attract women. The skill of getting into the head of my opponent when I played soccer became useful as I told a lot of these girls many things that made them commit to me for long periods of time. I convinced them to conduct illegal acts and risk their lives for me, either transporting or selling drugs for me. What power I had. I didn't know at the time how to use it positively for the good of my people.

I made so much money as a teenager that I did not know what to do with it. But one thing I knew was not to flaunt it. I had a nice car with dealer stacked rims and tires, nothing stylish or shiny to avoid attention while in the streets. I did not play loud music when driving to avoid attention, and I always had a female in the car as a form of distraction. My chains and bracelet were hardly exposed, and my earrings were expensive but small. As much as possible, I tried not to be seen by the eyes of those who may consider me as a drug dealer or gangster. I choose the name 'CJ' to be called in the streets. No one knew me as Pete A. Kennedy. The life I lived then required me to change a lot.

♦ ♦ ♦

My good friend and world-known leader John Maxwell, in his book *Developing the Leader Within You* quotes "Not all change is improvement - but without change there can be no improvement". - But Without Change There Can Be No Improvement'. This quote has made me view and accept change with a different mindset. I now understand that there are some changes we go through in life that are inevitable. For example, aging and teething. We must understand in life how to accept and embrace change while seeking growth opportunities within each change we experience. As I interact with others and listen to many of my clients, I have discovered that individuals fear changes due to the type of leadership they have been exposed to.

Here is an example: I was a part of a church that started in the garage of the founder's home. Bishop Lyttle Sr. had emigrated from England. Today this church sits on its own property servicing the community of Fort Lauderdale. When Bishop Lyttle died, some members gave resistance to the new pastor who was his eldest son, Bishop Lyttle Jr. He was thinking big and wanted to do things differently. Many who resisted wanted Bishop Lyttle Jr. to keep things the same. During this transition, I saw people leave the church due to the different leadership styles. They did not want change.

The new pastor wanted to bring a modern look to the church. He wanted to develop and implement new evangelistic methods and improve the music within the church. Now to me, these were all great improvements based on his vision, but others felt differently and left. I strongly recommend you embrace change and allow the leader to share and implement their process. After you observe, you will be able to identify whether their system or process works for you. Today, this church is successfully impacting the community of Fort Lauderdale by feeding the poor and providing knowledge and resources to those in need to improve their lives.

I learned from one of my leaders years ago, that one must inspect what they expect. To inspect your results as a leader, visibility is needed. Just being present is visible, but that is not the visibility I am talking about. It is essential to have a positive presence within the lives of those you lead and inspire. Visibility is connecting, inspiring, and guiding those you lead, even your children.

How do I become visible within the lives of those you lead and inspire? Start by sharing those stories you have set aside to highlight your message as a leader. When you allow those you lead and inspire to get to know you, you help them understand your thought process. This allows your audience to get comfortable. Depending on their behavior style, they will soon start to share and seek leadership from you. A critical part of the visibility step is to remain consistent. Consistency will give those you lead a chance to buy into your vision that is regularly displayed in front of their eyes.

There is a quote that says, "Whenever you discover your passion, you never work another day in your life." I must say this statement is true. For the last 14 years, I have been living a fulfilled life through my passions: to teach, coach, train, and speak. I have connected with my students, and they always attempted to give 110%. They loved to hear my stories, and I noticed they would produce more after I shared a story in class every morning.

My mother taught me that pen and paper is powerful. It always speaks the truth. She would always encourage me to write things down, no matter how simple they were. I did and started to share with others how much I loved teaching, coaching, training, and speaking.

I would encourage one to put in place a commitment system around goals and aspirations. Let it be known to your loved ones and friends. This behavior has led me to confidently say: leaders, stand firm in your beliefs and what is right. My mother never waived her values for my lifestyle, she did not agree with it and made it clear. This was a huge lesson I learned. Leadership is integrity, honesty, and, at times, being vulnerable. Let us lead our families and loved ones by showing them how things are done and learning with them along the way.

♦ ♦ ♦

By now, my mother and family were totally aware of my lifestyle. I had moved out of the house and purchased my own car.

While I was selling drugs, my mother remained prayerful and worked two jobs. She worked at Home Depot as a cashier and at the Mather Nursing home as a nursing aid. For years she held both jobs. This was a well-educated woman from Jamaica who had worked for the Prime Minister Attorney's office. Her studies in Jamaica were not accepted here in the States. This meant that at her age, she had to enroll for the GED, which she passed. Unfortunately, she was still unable to get a better job. This was the reason my Dad went back to Jamaica because he could not start over after working at Jamaica Public Service (JPS) for over 25 years.

My mother was totally in disagreement with my lifestyle, and I kept her totally away from it for her safety. She showed me tough love and kept praying for me. Every opportunity she got, she reminded me. Her behavior was the intention. My mother was planting the seeds of love and support whilst in disagreement with my lifestyle. This strategy worked because of her consistency. I would think of my mother every time I was in the streets, and I became even more careful as I operated in the GD community. To keep myself safe, I went as far as buying a stick shift (manual) car, so no one could drive my car. In the gang, we would drive each other's cars. Fortunately, most of the gangsters could not drive a manual car, so they left my car alone.

I decided to give mommy some money one day, and I left $3k on her coffee table for her. Although this money would help my mother financially, she wanted no part of the life I was living. She covered the money with crochet for three weeks and did not touch it.

She called and said, "My God provides, I don't need your dirty money, Pete, but I love you son, and I am praying for you to change. This is not what I wanted for your life."

She would then warn me that if I did not come and pick up the money, she would give it to a friend. The following week I went to pick up the money and saw it in the same place I left it untouched; she covered it with the crochet.

She was a loving but stern woman who believed in standing firm in what she thought was right. But she always acted in a peaceful manner while seeking growth in every opportunity. A true leader in many ways, but she was leading men who had different behavior styles. During all this, I was arrested twice while living that lifestyle: once for cocaine and the other for marijuana.

The last time I got arrested, the warden who processed me looked me in the eyes and said, "Son, you don't belong here."

I felt loved and challenged at the same time and have never been arrested since.

Leaders stand firm in their beliefs and what is right. My mother never waived her values for my lifestyle, which was a huge lesson I learned. Being vulnerable, honest, and trustworthy are all great leadership qualities to develop. Let us lead our families and loved ones in a true manner by showing them how things are done.

When a Man Loves

Activity

Step 1: Past Purpose/Commitments

Looking back at your childhood, would you say you felt called to a purpose?

Y/N

If so, what was it?

For Y: List 3-5 commitments you had in life

Example: School, Church, Friendship

#. _____

Did you commit to it?

Y/N

Was it aligned with your purpose?

Y/N

If yes, how? _____

If no, how did it affect you?

_____

For N: List 3-5 commitments you would like to commit to in life

Example: School, Church, Community Programs, Organizations, Friendship, Hobbies, etc.

#. _____

Did you commit to it?

Y/N

Did it inspire you towards any kind of purpose?

Y/N

If yes, how? _____

If no, how did it benefit you? _____

49

Step 2: Present Purpose and Commitments
Looking at your life today, what would you say your purpose is?
_____

List 3-5 commitments you had in life.
Example: School, Church, Community Programs, Organizations, Friendship, Hobbies
#. _____
Is it aligned with your purpose?
Y/N
If yes, how? _____
If no, how does that affect you? _____
_____

Do you stay committed to it?
Y/N
If Y, Why? _____
If N, do you feel called to leave?
_____
What would be a better commitment?
_____
_____

My mother has always been encouraging and shared from a visionary perspective. My mother then made a statement that I would understand later.

She said, "Stumps yuh decide yuh a man now, mommy will always support you in any good and be here for you. You can continue to live with mommy once you're living an upright life."

I interpreted this incorrectly at the time. I thought that she was telling me to leave the house. This was because I called the GD gang my family now. I was known as a 'GD', selling the white boys crack & cocaine and living a gangster life wearing my black and red secretly.

Chapter 4

Losing Daddy, Gaining Brothers

(Leadership and Opportunities for Growth and Trust)

With Tupac blasting in the car, I was on my way to the block as usual. It was work time. I was dressed in a long-sleeve polo shirt with jeans, Nike Air Jordans, and a hat to match. I was ready. I pulled into my normal parking spot on Howard Street, my block, and then entered the building to my girlfriend's apartment to drop off my drugs. I kept them there for safety and easy access. It was just a trip upstairs and back, selling eight balls and ounces all night.

It was 2000, and at this time, Marlon was living in Jamaica with daddy. Mom and I were in Chicago. Standing on the street corner, my phone rang. It was Marlon, we spoke on a regular basis, so it wasn't unusual for him to call. What was not normal was the news Marlon had to share with me: our dad had died. I had just seen my father two weeks prior; he had traveled to Chicago for his normal six-month visit. But I did not know that would be our last time together.

This was terrifying to me. During this time, I can say my dad and I communicated as adults. I was a young man on my own, making money on my own, but still, he exemplified no leadership. He accepted my lifestyle, unlike mommy. He never brought up the topic. When a man loves, he protects. They communicate with transparency, honest, loyal, and, build trust with those they influence. This lifestyle requires practice!

After receiving the news, I sat on the sidewalk and cried to myself! If my dad can die suddenly, here I am out in the streets, selling drugs and in dangerous territory. I am the walking dead. I reflected on my life, sitting on that block. My life flashed in front of me. I knew I needed a change. But where and how do I change was the question.

A week later, I flew to Jamaica for the burial of my dad. Family, close friends, and our community attended in huge numbers. So many people came that many had to stand outside. At the church service, I saw a young man with the Kennedy family signature. My dad and all his kids had similar nose structures, which signified the Kennedys. This little boy had our signature. With all the distractions, I mentioned nothing to Marlon or my mother. But as we were getting ready to lay my dad to rest, I saw the little boy again at the burial ground.

With this reminder, I said to my mother that this little boy looks like us. She told me to behave myself. A few minutes later, I discovered the little boy was my youngest brother. His name was Carlyle O'Shane Kennedy. The puzzle did not stop there. Later that evening, I met another brother who was born directly after me. His name was Mark Kennedy. I finally figured out where the additional loaves of bread were going.

I love my brothers and sisters, but my dad was unable to provide for me 100% in the way a man should because of his other children. I was able to close my curiosity, I was not upset. When my dad died, he had a total of seven children with five different women. Marcia and Olivine, the eldest, shared the same mother, Nikki had a separate mother, Marlon and I shared the same mother (Mrs. Joyce), while Mark and Carlyle had different mothers.

Immediately at the funeral, my mother displayed leadership qualities: Mark and Carlyle were accepted by her with open arms, no questions asked. Since my father's passing I have traveled to Jamaica a few times. Each time I made sure I spent some time with Mark. Mark and I would go to Hillshire beach to eat fry-fish and see festivals. We visited the mineral bath in St. Thomas, where hot mineral water springs from the rocks in the mountains. We spent a lot of time getting to know each other. These were memories I will never forget. I am glad I was able to create them with my brother Mark until he migrated to the United Kingdom. Carlyle was unable to come with us on those road journeys with Mark and me because he was a little boy. Carlyle lives in Canada with his mom. I only met Carlyle in person once, but Mark and I were able to develop a close relationship over the years. This was the beginning of me realizing that leadership is love.

As I sat on the plane back to Chicago, I wondered how could I change this lifestyle of the gang and drug selling. I wanted out. I thought about finding a job and starting to work a regular 9 to 5. I thought about opening a business since I had some money. But, what business? With no resolution, I landed in Chicago. My phone lit up with voicemails and text messages from clients. Right back at it again.

Standing on Howard Street, I started to wonder how I was going to make this change. I walked to the convenience store on the street. The owner of it was named Coolie man. He and I had created a great relationship. I was very respectful whenever I purchased something from his store, and I respected his business. Coolie man knew I was a hustler, but he never saw me in action due to the respect I had for him. He knew it. Whenever I visited his store, we would talk about the Chicago Bulls, the Cubs, or whenever I played soccer.

About the second week back in town, one day Coolie man said to me, "Do you wanna buy this store? I am moving to New York."

In total shock, I turned to him and said, "What you just say?"

"You heard me, do you want to buy this store?"

"Me?"

He said, "Yes, you!"

"How much?"

He gave me his price, and I said let me think it over and get back to you. This was showing me that I was above the gangster lifestyle, and Coolie man saw better and bigger in me. This was an opportunity. I mentioned this idea to my gang leaders. I recommended that we invest in real estate and start owning the community we hustle in. With ownership, the gang would have more power and leverage to our advantage. But they thought my idea was too much. I was told we are GD for life, and gang banging is what we do. We don't go buy real estate. This was the confirmation I needed to change, and this lifestyle was not me. I did not purchase the store.

All was going well in school, but I could not seem to find the solution to my change. I had no mentor or leadership guidance to seek direction or support. The only leaders I saw were also a part of the gang. I enjoyed the money I made, the cars I drove, the jewelry I could buy, and the women I dated. How could I change and not lose all these advantages? So, I decided to switch from selling cocaine to selling marijuana. The transition to weed was easy because I smoked it and had positive views on the herb from a little boy in Jamaica. In addition to the transition to selling weed, I also became a Rastafarian and grew out my hair. Was selling weed better, no. I was still selling drugs. But I felt it had a less harmful impact on someone and weed was not as damaging.

The demand for weed was way less than cocaine, so I was not required to be on the block as much. This was good for me. I

When a Man Loves

was slowly making the changes. My father's death propelled my life change. I no longer wanted to hurt people with cocaine. But I did not want to completely give up the lifestyle because of the money and women that came with it. I started having leadership qualities come into my life, but I had no positive influence to help develop these skills.

♦ ♦ ♦

Repeatedly throughout this book, you will hear me reference this quote because I truly believe it. "Leadership is influence, nothing more, nothing less." It is quoted by a friend and world-known leader John Maxwell. After all my years of studying leadership, my quote is, 'Leadership is Love, Love is Leadership.'

There are many qualities of a leader that require practice to be used effectively. These qualities, if exposed to a child from an early age through life examples and stories, will surely set up a child for success. Even if these qualities are implemented at a later stage in life, they will also bring success. Implementing these behaviors will set up an individual for success. Look at the table below; it provides descriptions of different leadership qualities. Complete the table with a description of each leadership quality.

Attributes of a Leader

Attribute of a Leader	Description
	Effective leaders take calculated risks when necessary to achieve their objectives. If a mistake is made, the effective leader will learn from the mistake and use it as an opportunity to explore other avenues.
	Because they know who they are, effective leaders are also aware of their weaknesses. They only make promises they can follow through on.
	Leaders convey an aura of honesty in both their professional and their personal lives.
	Effective leaders know what they want to do and have the strength of character to pursue their objectives in the face of opposition and spite of failures. The effective leader establishes achievable goals.
	The effective leader is dedicated to his or her charge and will work assiduously on behalf of those following. The leader gives himself or herself entirely to the task when it is necessary.
	Leaders Listen! This is the most important attribute of all, listen to your followers.
	Effective leaders believe passionately in their goals. They have a positive outlook on who they are, and they love what they do. Their passion for life is a guiding star for others to follow, because they radiate promise!
	Effective leaders earn the trust of their followers and act on behalf of their followers.

55

Now, let me see how well you completed the worksheet.

Attributes of a Leader

Attribute of a Leader	Description
RISK	Effective leaders take calculated risks when necessary to achieve their objectives. If a mistake is made, the effective leader will learn from the mistake and use it as an opportunity to explore other avenues.
INTEGRITY	Because they know who they are, effective leaders are also aware of their weaknesses. They only make promises they can follow through on.
HONESTY	Leaders convey an aura of honesty in both their professional and their personal lives.
VISION	Effective leaders know what they want to do and have the strength of character to pursue their objectives in the face of opposition and spite of failures. The effective leader establishes achievable goals.
DEDICATION	The effective leader is dedicated to his or her charge and will work assiduously on behalf of those following. The leader gives himself or herself entirely to the task when it is necessary.
LISTENING	Leaders Listen! This is the most important attribute of all, listen to your followers.
PASSION	Effective leaders believe passionately in their goals. They have a positive outlook on who they are, and they love what they do. Their passion for life is a guiding star for others to follow, because they radiate promise!
TRUST	Effective leaders earn the trust of their followers and act on behalf of their followers.

Now that we have the complete list, it is time to act and start practicing. PRACTICE! PRACTICE! PRACTICE! I believe all these previously mentioned experiences are leadership growth opportunities.

When I discovered my brothers at my dad's funeral, my growth opportunity as a leader was accepting them and treating them as equal: **TRUST**. That was a behavior I learned from my mother as I observed her loving, caring, and communicating with Mark and Carlyle as if they were her own. Having this experience in my personal life made it easy for me to emulate the same traits professionally. I now accept people for who they are and trust them. This characteristic has allowed me to connect, inspire, and lead effectively.

I get asked all the time, "How do you get along with everyone?"

The answer is easy: I give people I meet 100% trust and the opportunity to enhance themselves with this new relationship. A huge part of being an effective and successful leader is PRACTICE! PRACTICE! PRACTICE!

Leaders need to take risks. People shy away from leadership because of this; they do not want to take the **RISK** of leading others. But have you ever thought that being a parent is taking a risk, maybe not? This is because of the stigma society places behind these words and their content. Most things in our daily routines are risky. Driving in cars is risky: it is not guaranteed that we will get back home. Getting on an aircraft is risky, we do not know the pilot's state of mind, do we? Every day, there are plenty of risks we take that we do not see as risks anymore.

Why not step out and live your passion, why not take that risk too? I believe growth comes from a place of being uncomfortable or doing something uncomfortable. Remember the first time you drove a car how uncomfortable you felt, and the risk you took being on the road to practice driving. No one knew you were new at this, and they took the risk of driving with you on the road. But after a few months, you got comfortable, and driving became way easier.

A lobster only grows when it gets uncomfortable within its hard shell. It does not expand until the lobster replaces its shell. It is at that time the lobster goes below a rock to replace its shell, so it can grow. As humans, we do not have to wait until we get uncomfortable in ourselves to grow. We can put ourselves in uncomfortable situations to propel our own growth. If you can afford to put yourself in an uncomfortable situation repeatedly, your growth will happen.

◆ ◆ ◆

Rastafarianism became a part of my new lifestyle. I grew my hair out and started to listen to more of my culture's music, like Bob Marley, Capleton, Sizzla, Anthony B, and Tony Rebel. Culture music was different than dancehall because they spoke about upliftment in life and positivity. But my lifestyle change was still missing true and effective leadership. I was trying to figure this out by myself.

By late 2000, I got some help. My best friend Kizzy had moved to Chicago too. I never really established any close friends like Kizzy. I was so happy to have Kizzy with me. We were in the States together. This was one of the dreams we discussed on the street corners of Jamaica before I left. I made a commitment that he was not going to get involved in drug selling and the GD family. I wanted to keep him clean. His focus was to play soccer and stay in college.

He got enrolled in Kennedy College in Chicago (how coincidental that the name of the school is my surname). He played one season of soccer and could not return the following season due to an injury. We both grew our dreadlocks and studied the life of Haile Selassie, the person Rastafarians worship, and the Rastafarian culture. We stopped eating pork and beef and ate more seafood as our diet. When you saw me, you saw him! I loved and enjoyed every moment we spent together.

Due to his injury, Kizzy left school. Living the lives as Rastafarians, we decided to start writing and recording music. I purchased a Windows Gateway PC with all the top music and recording features and got a mic. We began writing and recording our own music for fun. This is where my love for speaking was reactivated.

In the beginning, we sang over tracks we downloaded from the internet. Later we found a local artist who started to create our own tracks for us as we continued to write and record. Here were two young men trying to improve themselves, but we were still lacking the leadership and guidance from exemplary men. The one thing that did not change, and got worse after Kizzy arrived, was having multiple women or girlfriends. What I loved the most was Kizzy supported my education. He would wake me up in the morning and helped with schoolwork when needed. This made it easy to stay focused in school.

Kizzy was a wake-up call for me and kept me on track. One day, I was at school early, in the cafeteria, grabbing a small hot chocolate and a banana before class. As I paid for my items at the cash register, my black and red bandana in my back pocket was recognized by a Latin King. He was a gang member named Jose from a different group. He approached me and threw up his gang sign. He knew we were rivals. The first person I thought of was my mother: I could not afford to get kicked out of school because of a gang.

So, I approached him carefully and displayed means of peace with my hands in the air and said, "Hey, let's do this after class in the parking lot. We both will get expelled, fighting in the cafeteria."

Surprisingly, he said, "Ok."

When my classes were done, I went to the parking lot and waited for his classes to end. While waiting, I rolled and lit a spliff (a Jamaican blunt) in my car. With all this time to think while waiting, I came up with a plan. I planned to share with my rival gang member that our goal at school is to learn and not to waste money, which we try to avoid as gang members. We can try to avoid each other and respect each other while in school. That was the plan!

Forty-five minutes later, I saw him coming. I exited my car and stood outside, so he could see me. He was approaching fast, upset, and angry. But I soon realized it had nothing to do with our interaction earlier because he looked straight through me as he got closer as if he forgot who I was. After speaking with him, he was upset about an issue he had in class. I saw this as an opportunity to suggest peace and to help, just like I have seen my mother display as a leader. I immediately shared my plan with him.

"Hey man, I don't know you, and you don't know me. But it is obvious we have the same goal for learning and educating ourselves. I do not think it is wise we bring our gang lives to school to destroy it for ourselves and the other students."

Surprisingly, he said, "I like that plan, I just didn't want you to think I was weak."

Soon after, I offered him a puff of my spliff, and then I offered to get him help with his classes.

He coughed, an after effect from puffing my spliff, and he asked, "Where did you get this stuff from?'

I responded, "I got that, you like it?"

He said yes, and I reached in my car and gave him some for his personal use.

I introduced him to a few friends at school to assist him with his schoolwork, which later he improved drastically. Months later, Jose and I developed a good personal and business relationship.

He was impressed and liked the weed I gave him that day in the parking lot at school. He later became one of my clients seeking to purchase huge amounts of weed. He became my biggest client as I transitioned to selling marijuana. In our first business transaction, he purchased 15 pounds of weed. With that kind of purchase bi-weekly, I did not need to hustle on the block anymore or contact any of my GD friends. I was making money without them and did not need them anymore. I used my leadership skills to influence my new friend to see the bigger picture, which later turned into a close friendship.

We kept our relationship a secret, as it was not the norm to create a close friendship with someone from an opposite gang. My schoolmate and I spent a lot of quality time together, which allowed us to learn more about each other's life. All this time God was looking out for me as I strived to change my life. I am not saying God supported the lifestyle that I lived, but he kept me safe while I derailed from his purpose for a moment. Yes, I was influencing others but not in the positive way I was ordained to yet.

A friend of mine affiliated with the GD family called me one day. He shared with me that he had a way for us to make some money. His idea was for us to set up my schoolmate to get robbed whenever he was coming next to get his bi-weekly product. I was shocked and amazed.

But I immediately rejected the idea and responded, "That is not going to happen."

I was not interested in the idea and did not want to know why he was thinking like that. Knowing his mindset, I stopped including him in the bi-weekly sale where he could sell about five pounds to my schoolmate. This was another sign that this lifestyle was not for me, and I needed out. There was no reason to rob my schoolmate. My fellow GD friend was upset that I was not in agreement with the robbery, and I made it clear it was not going to happen. He nor any of my GD friends were thinking of my school, my mom, or me. They were thinking of themselves. Here, I am exemplifying another leadership quality standing firm on what is right. All I had was my integrity while in the wrong environment with no guidance.

Activity

- Past Leaders
- Look at Chapter 3's Worksheet
- You shared 3-5 commitments
- I want you to think of people who were part of those commitments.
- People who were part of your life during that time.
- Who is an example of each of the following leadership attributes?
- Risk: _____
- Integrity: _____
- Honesty: _____
- Vision: _____
- Dedication: _____
- Listening: _____
- Passion: _____
- Trust: _____
- Present Leadership
- Reflection
- How are you exampling the following attributes?
- Alternatively, if you feel that you aren't exampling any of them, where you can you start?
- Short Response
- Risk: _____

_____

_____

_____

_____

- Integrity: _____
  _____
  _____
  _____
  _____

- Honesty: _____
  _____
  _____
  _____
  _____

- Vision: _____
  _____
  _____
  _____
  _____

- Dedication: _____
  _____
  _____
  _____
  _____

- Listening: _____
  _____
  _____
  _____
  _____

- Passion: _____
  _____
  _____
  _____
  _____

- Trust: _____
  _____
  _____
  _____
  _____

Chapter 5

Approaching the Honeycomb

(Wavering Integrity, Uncomfortable Conversations, and Consistency)

Since DeVry did not offer any sports, I continued to play soccer at the club level in Chicago. I represented a Belizean team. I became the captain of the team and was involved with management decisions. I quickly incorporated Kizzy into our squad. It felt so good having a familiar face on the soccer field. We knew how each other played, which was a bonus on the field. Now in Chicago, Kizzy and I would drive to soccer practice. This was a contrast from when we were younger in Jamaica, walking back and forth from soccer. No more being chased by dogs in a gully! That season we won the championship. It was an exciting feeling to have Kizzy beside me on this journey. Compared to high school, it felt amazing winning with him this time around.

In the final semester in college, my excitement arose as it got closer to graduation. I had longed for the experience to walk across a stage as a graduate since I did not have a ceremony in high school.

Professor Jones from our computer programming class had given us a project, and we were assigned to groups. Within my group, I was given my task. My group was scheduled to meet on Saturday to work on our project. As I was preparing to leave to meet with my group to work on our project, Kizzy asked if he could come with me? I shared with him I was going to a group meeting, and it would take some time. I did not want to be rushed. It was crunch time! So if he could abide by those guidelines, then I was ok with him coming with me.

A few minutes later, after thinking, I changed my decision to no. I shared with him I did not want to be rushed. He would be more comfortable at home than sitting in a lab for hours with no strategic plan. He insisted on coming, and I insisted he did not. After a few minutes, we agreed he would stay home. Knowing my lifestyle, I communicated consistently with Kizzy just to keep him away from the gang lifestyle I was currently living. Kizzy lived with me the whole time he was in Chicago.

That Saturday morning, one of my girlfriends had slept the night over and at the apartment in the north side of Chicago. There were rules and guidelines we created for our house, as Kizzy knew about my lifestyle. Some of the rules were the bedroom curtains and the shades should always remain closed/shut. This was where we counted our cash and prepared our drugs; we could not afford for our neighbors to see what we were doing. Another rule was if we did not expect any guest, no matter what, do not open the door. It was not the first time Crystal, one of my girlfriends, was spending the night at the apartment. She was aware of the house rules as well.

As I left my apartment, I saw one of my fellow gang members in the back apartment. I did not think anything of it because there was another apartment building attached. That is where they would visit other clients of theirs. So, I proceeded to get to my car and got ready to leave for school. As I prepared to drive out of my parking spot, a Geo Tracker (small two-door SUV at the time) pulled up next to me and blocked me from exiting.

Two men exited the vehicle with guns. One pulled me out of the car and placed me in the back seat of my car while one attempted to drive off. He could not move the car because it was a manual shift. Realizing he could not drive my car, they decided to place me in their car, which was too small. But they had no choice at this point. I was placed in the back of a Geo Tracker with another GD member while the other two were upfront. They demanded my money and the marijuana they thought I had in the house. I refused to give up anything, so they started to get annoyed and angry.

Since I was studying the Rastafarian faith, one of my new habits was to read the Bible every day. Two of the three guys were from my direct GD family and the other was from the GD family on the south side of Chicago. The men continued to demand money and marijuana from me, shocked. In dismay, my only response was to pray.

I started reciting the 23rd Psalms, *"The Lord is my shepherd, I shall not want, He maketh me to lie down in green pastures: he leadeth me beside the still waters. He restoreth my soul…"*

Bang! Bang! Two shots went off, seconds later I realized I was shot in the arm.

The guy in the passenger seat had fired two shots, and I was hit between my elbow and wrist. I looked at the faces of the driver and the guy in the back seat with me: this was a total shock to everyone. I started to feel pain, and then the left side of my body began to feel numb. I still withheld the cash and marijuana, so they gave up and decided to drop me off at the Honeycomb. I have never been there before, but the Honeycomb was known as the place you would be taken and never to return or seen again. Now I got scared, and so was everyone in the car.

I was getting weak and bleeding from my left arm. I fell back in the seat. On the way to the Honeycomb, they changed their minds. I felt the small SUV coming to a stop, and they threw me out of the car on the side of the street and stripped me of my cell phone. At this time, had no idea where I was, and the left side of my body was numb. I found the last bits of strength that I had, and I checked my surroundings. I realized I was in front of someone's door.

I crawled up and banged on the door, seeking someone's attention. Then I heard the inches of the door open. My face was on the ground and I was feeling weak.

I saw the light from the inside of the apartment, I asked, "Please help me."

In shock, the lady at the door screamed, then came the rest of the people in the apartment. They turned me over, and the young man who was holding me said, "CJ what happened?"

Struggling to open my eyes as I got weaker from the blood I was losing, I recognized the voice of a young teenage boy name 'Zion'. Zion hung around the other high school boys I would hang with sometimes. He was of average height with curly hair and dark skin. His sister flirted with me whenever we saw each other, and it was a family I truly just had a love and care for. They were all genuine people!

Later, I would provide as much as I could to the boys about the life of drug dealing and gang banging. This was with the intent to discourage them from getting involved. This is where I would gather these young men and just share as we did on the street corners in Jamaica. This time I had power and control to guide the conversation. What I preached was a little better than what Kizzy and I heard on the street corners in Jamaica. A few minutes later, Zion and his sister took me to Evanston Hospital. Kizzy and my girlfriend took me home after I was released from the hospital. This made me realize I needed a change. But, did I?

♦ ♦ ♦

While change is inevitable and should be embraced, there are certain attributes we should develop where it does not change. Once the attribute of integrity is mastered, one will easily connect and develop trust with others. An effective leader should always strive to practice integrity and seek to do the right thing. As we identified in chapter 4, one of the attributes of a leader is having integrity. This means the leader is aware of their weakness and only makes promises they can follow through on.

Earlier in my career, integrity was missing from my relationships, both personally and professionally. Now I understood the importance of integrity. Every new relationship was an opportunity for me to practice and develop this quality. As I got more comfortable and understood how to be a man of integrity, it started to impact the existing relationships in my life. Just like all other leadership qualities, integrity must be practiced. When these behaviors are embedded in the subconscious mind, this allows a leader to live and react with integrity when needed.

Years later, in 2005 when I was in Florida, on the journey of leadership, I held the role of youth director. This role truly developed my integrity and is an accredited behavior. This will allow you to influence youths positively. Otherwise, youths will be respectful to you as an adult, but you will not influence their lives as a leader. It was always rewarding when I witnessed the expression on a youth's face whenever I came through on my promises. It was encouraging along the way.

Over time, I was known as the leader who would support my youths to the very end. I would show up at events and practices just to support them. I would be their biggest cheerleader, making noise on the sideline. Yes, I am that parent, guardian, or supporter! I would immediately correct when they were wrong but faster to forgive and move forward. Integrity, along with other leadership qualities, allowed me to connect with my youths. I would use these quality moments to influence them in being the best at whatever they desired to be or would just to listen if they needed to talk.

In leadership, all the attributes are aligned with each other in some way or another. Developing a quality of integrity has a direct impact on the quality of communication. To be a person of integrity, you must communicate what you can get done and what you cannot. For the things you cannot get done, allow others to do it who are good at it or who are willing to get it done. For example, one of the weakness of an Entertainer is to be organized. I have improved this behavior of mine, but I have someone in my business who handles all of my appointments, etc., to keep me and my clients on track. This person does a better job than I do because they love what they do, while I can focus on speaking, teaching, coaching and training, which is what I love to do. In this manner, a leader can inspect what they expect and communicate along the way. What has helped me tremendously is having an accountability partner and support system. My accountability partner's name is Michael.

Here are a few questions for you:
- Do you have support in your life?
- Are you surrounded by people who will hold you accountable?
- If you fall, will they aid in your recovery?
- Will they hold you true to your integrity/values/beliefs?

When you are comfortable communicating and doing it consistently, you will be in a good position to communicate on a subject that is uncomfortable to you.

What I have done is practice this quote from my brother Marlon, "We must get comfortable with uncomfortable conversations."

When he first said this, it marinated for a few minutes in my spirit. I immediately put it into action and began practicing at home. I started talking to friends and family. We would have a discussion around topics like sex, what type of partner are you, do you have a high sex drive or no? What is your goal towards intimacy with the relationship and finance? What happened to me was as I practiced, those I lead, and those who were just witnesses were able to see the growth and difference within me. That's because I lead by example. Practicing integrity leads to better communication, which leads to one leading by example.

This behavior has proven time and time again to enhance relationships. There will be better communication between you and those you lead or interact with. One thing I did was express to my family and friends that I am a man of my word. Every time I said something, I followed through. I immediately saw the change in those around me as the trust grew and communication became tremendously better.

As leaders, we must master the art of being comfortable with uncomfortable conversations. Many of those uncomfortable conversations will set you up as a leader for success. Keep in mind uncomfortable does not mean discussing the difficult topics all the time. It can also be topics that we are discussing for the first time like business transactions for a new entrepreneur or pitching the idea of a sale to a potential investor. Practice! Practice! Practice! That is the key to getting comfortable with uncomfortable conversations.

I strive to display the same behaviors at work and at home. I do not believe we should be living two lives, one at home and another at work. This causes people to not function in their full capacity and can create stress. Who loses here is your family while your job gains from the time you lock in at work. The moment I walk into my home, I am ready and cannot wait to interact with my family.

Like the leadership qualities we have discussed so far, consistency carries the weight of them all. The visibility of our leadership involves consistency because while we are present, those we lead are constantly observing our behavior. This includes when we interact with others and when we speak. I learned a method from one of my prior managers called P.I.E.: performance, image, and exposure. This method has consistently allowed me to seize growth opportunities while opening the doors for others to refer me to like-minded people.

The method works like this:

- Performance: Everyone is familiar with LeBron James, whether you are a basketball fan or not. The reason for this is because "he is known as a top performer." The team will more than likely get to the championship finals, and jersey sales would increase. These are all great things that come with having a LeBron James on your team. The same goes for me when I am in a workplace, I first focus on performing at the highest level possible. Whenever I speak or teach on this method, I always share this theory. At the top executive level, one of the important components of an organization is performing. I always strive for that level of performance. Leaders will get to know you by your name when it consistently appears at the top of their report before they ever lay eyes on you. This is performance!

- Image: This is all about how you look and the image you want others to have of you. Your attire should mirror your personality. Here is what I did when I became a Training Assistant at T-Mobile in 2006. I wore casual jeans and a button-down shirt Monday through Thursday. On Fridays, I would wear a polo shirt or a t-shirt. When I transitioned to Trainer, Supervisor, and all other leadership roles, I wore dress pants or slacks and a button-down shirt tucked in to work. Fridays I wore casual jeans with a polo shirt or t-shirt with a sweater over it. I did this for years, which created an image for my leadership. I was taken more seriously compared to my peers. Whenever I speak or teach on this method, I always share the theory that your attire should speak to the level of leadership you would like to display as well as receive.

- Exposure: This is your sales moment or selling point. I remember while in Chicago, I worked as a salesperson for a small company selling alarm systems door to door. We would meet at the office, and the company had vehicles that would take us out to the communities and drop us off in different locations. I would walk through the neighborhood, trying to sell these alarm systems to homeowners. Trust me, it was a job I performed poorly. I sold one alarm system. But later in life, I realized that I must understand who I am to be the best salesperson. This drives growth, success, and enhances relationships. Whenever I speak or teach on this method, I always share this theory about exposure. No one can sell you as you do. Your executive leadership team will know you by name after you consistently perform at the highest level and will one day get the opportunity to meet you. No one will know when that day is, due to impromptu visits. If it happens last minute, will you be prepared? I always encourage leaders to create an infomercial of themselves to share with others when asked who are you?

Also, many leaders are not prepared to take advantage of the statement: I've heard a lot about you. This is your exposure moment. I believe this is the moment a leader gets to confirm the performance seen on paper and connect. As a leader in the banking industry, our regional manager was in the area and decided to visit us. This was to specifically meet me after seeing all the top performance for weeks on paper. Because of the consistency in my image, he was impressed with my attire. I received a compliment and was offered lunch. I had my information prepared ahead of time, when he asked me to tell them about myself. I was ready to respond. Leaving impressed and connected, he later offered me an opportunity for growth.

My life surrounds the model of P.I.E. I suggest you discover a model that works for you. If not, use P.I.E.

◆ ◆ ◆

After three weeks of recovery, Kizzy and I had decided we were going to retaliate and kill the person who shot me. It was time to put in place our plan. Susan, one of my girlfriends, was affiliated with the gang, and she was tasked to be our lookout. Whenever she saw those guys we were looking for, her job was to call me immediately. But we could never seem to catch them every time we heard they were on the block. At one point, I called Susan disloyal. I sometimes treated her badly because she would not produce the information we needed.

A month went by, and Kizzy and I were unsuccessful in locating these guys. One day, Kizzy and I were smoking in the living room. We had just finished devotion, and it was time for breakfast. As we prepared breakfast and chatted amongst ourselves like we always do, Kizzy said to me, "Stumps, yuh know sey yuh fi leave dem bwoy alone."

I was shocked and said, "What?"

He said, "Yes man. I understand you got shot, but you still have your arm."

I just needed to go to therapy to strengthen the arm. He continued to say you have a lot ahead of you and these guys are not worth it for blood on your hands when there so much more we can accomplish. Take it as a learning lesson and testimony.

I could not believe what I was hearing, but I said, "Yuh know what I am going to be obedient."

I then used this incident to leave the gang. Years later, I discovered obedience is better than sacrifice.

Activity

Hard Topics

- Write down 3-5 topics you avoid talking about

    1. _____
    2. _____
    3. _____
    4. _____
    5. _____

Short Response

For each topic...

- Write three things you are afraid of hearing.

    1. _____   A. _____

       B. _____

       C. _____

    2. _____   A. _____

       B. _____

       C. _____

3. _____ A. _____

   B. _____

   C. _____

4. _____ A. _____

   B. _____

   C. _____

5. _____ A. _____

   B. _____

   C. _____

BONUS: Pursue the words you need to hear.

For each topic…

Write down someone you know who can have this conversation with you.

Next time you see them, ask them if they'd be willing to go through this with you.

Better yet, reach out to them now.

1. _____
2. _____
3. _____
4. _____
5. _____

Chapter 6

The Secret Sauce to Life, Forgiveness

(The Secret Sauce to Life)

A few months earlier, Melanie had become pregnant. She sat me down to share the wonderful news. I was excited to become a dad because I made a choice: I would settle down with her and create a family. She continued to share that I may not be the father because she had cheated. She shared that she knew I was cheating and got tired of being alone sometimes and, had an affair as well. My joy turned to sorrow and quickly escalated to anger. But with the values that Mrs. Joyce instilled in me, which was to take care of my responsibilities, my response to her was, "I will be there for you and the child until birth because if she is mine, I do not want to miss the chance of being there as a dad. We will take a paternity test later."

Again, exemplifying leadership and not knowing. I was there the entire nine months and on the day of birth at the hospital as well. I witnessed the magnificent work of God through childbirth, so I named the child Jahnique. Which stands for Jah Is Unique!

October 25, 2002 was a day I longed to experience: graduation day. As I crossed the stage to collect my bachelor's degree, I felt accomplished and happy. That was not how I felt in high school. I was disappointed when I did not get to walk across the stage. But now I was able to experience the excitement, joy, and feeling of great accomplishment as I exited the stage. Have you ever smiled so much it hurts? That is how happy I was.

There was no other person to share this moment with but my mother. I hugged and thanked her so much for being loyal to her values and loving me unconditionally. I also invited Melanie to experience this joyous moment with me. I wanted my graduating to be a form of motivation for her to attain the same one day. This was me displaying leadership without me knowing it.

It was now time to celebrate my graduation, and I decided to go to the park where we all hung out. A few months prior Kizzy had moved to Boston with his girlfriend Samantha, who was pregnant and wanted to start his family. I was back on my own again. I stood in the park and celebrated my accomplishment with a few friends. No one in the GD family knew I was in school, much less celebrating my graduation. I kept it a secret. It was a silent or internal celebration. Only my family and Tony knew of this other lifestyle, and surprisingly Tony kept that a secret.

I had a drink of Hennessey in one hand and a spliff in the other feeling nice and mellow. Then I saw the guy who shot me approaching from the other side of the park. Shocked and scared, I froze and did not know what to do. As he got closer, my body began to shake. Now others started to observe what was happening. With no Kizzy as support, I was alone.

In total shock, he approached me and said, "CJ, please forgive me. Our intention was not to shoot you. But I am not sure what happened, and I am sorry."

In a surprise, I did not know what to say. The only response I had was, "I forgive you. It's alright."

Immediately my nice and mellow feeling went away, and I could not drink or smoke anymore. I left the park a few minutes shortly after that experience and went home because I was shocked at what happened. After all, I did not want to hang out with the guy who shot me. That night when I got home, I decided that was it truly final, I am leaving the gang and never went back to the park.

Back in early 2001, my mother had moved to South Florida because the weather in Chicago was impacting her arthritis, which ran in our family history. She encouraged me to move to Florida with her. Although she had her siblings, she wanted her youngest son nearby. I was hesitant to move because of all the horror stories I heard from friends who had visited Florida from Chicago. I didn't realize that these horror stories were through the goggles of a gangster and drug dealers, which I was no longer a part of. But I still did not make the move to Florida.

One afternoon I was preparing lunch and decided to take a nap before I ate. During my nap, I heard people screaming from the apartment building, I looked out my window and saw children falling from the sky. In shock, I jumped out of bed to look at what was happening. As I looked out the window, parents from the above floors were throwing their children through the windows downstairs to loved ones. This was because the basement of the apartment was on fire and elevators were not safe. There was too much smoke and darkness to take the stairs down.

I lived on the first floor, so within a few minutes I was heavily impacted by smoke and had to leave the apartment. Melanie had her apartment where she and my daughter resided. After sharing what had happened to my apartment, she told me I could not stay there with them. Somehow my behavior did not qualify me to stay with her during the time, so I had nowhere to live. After that, I slept in my car for two months. When my mother discovered this, she immediately contacted my uncle and asked if he could move me to Florida. She paid the expenses for me to move, and my uncle helped me packed what I had left from the smoked apartment. We left Chicago and drove to Florida in early 2003.

When God has a plan and intends to get it accomplished, He does. To have an impact on those around me, I needed to change my environment to build confidence and trust in my behavioral and leadership skills. Staying in Chicago, it would be difficult to accomplish my intended purpose because everyone knew me as a drug dealer and gang banger. I needed to change my environment and friends. South Florida was the place to embrace and develop the new Pete.

When I arrived in South Florida, my experience was different than those horror stories I heard from others in Chicago. I was no longer living a gangster life, so police and rival gangs were never an issue for me.

My favorite thing about South Florida is the weather: *the Sunshine State*. This reminded me of 'back a yaad' Jamaica. The scenery was different compared to Illinois. It was hot and sunny all year, and all the major fruits and vegetables I am familiar with from Jamaica were grown here. Now, it was just about an hour and a half flight back home to Jamaica: this was the place to be. I joined my mother and grandmother Mable.

I was elated for the change and looked forward to new adventures, learning the new culture, and meeting new people. I applied for many jobs and went on many interviews. But, no one would hire me.

During this one interview, the lady interviewing me said at the end, "Young man, you have a lot of potential and talent. Your hairstyle of choice is getting in the way, I suggest you get a haircut."

I left that interview and decided to cut my hair. I wanted to share that moment with my family because I knew how badly my mother wanted me to cut my hair. So, I decided to have my aunt Marcia cut my hair. While growing up in Jamaica as a boy she used to cut my hair all the time. After planning with my aunt that weekend, I went by her house and she cut my dreadlocks off. When I went home and walked into the house, my mom cried for joy. She wanted to see me succeed at the highest level and it was a pleasure to see her tears of joy.

At the next interview, I was offered a job. I later realized dreadlocks were accepted in Illinois as a style but not in Florida where it was associated with gangs. I no longer wanted to be associated with that lifestyle anymore. This was a call to adjust! I could feel my mother's love as she encouraged me to change more and strive for the best.

She would constantly remind me by saying, "Son, I have forgiven you for the past. All is well."

♦ ♦ ♦

Forgiveness on the path to success

Forgiveness impacts all individuals in a positive way. This allows people to grow, if they desire to. I have witnessed this personally by forgiving the man who shot me and almost took my life. Since that day, I have been able to seize some great opportunities because my mind is free and open. It is no longer burdened with anger or resentment. When you portray this attitude others see it. This puts individuals in a position to want to work with you or refer you for the things you do well. I do not take anything personally as long as an individual does not harm my family or me physically. This approach allows me to forgive others and sets the tone for me to communicate and influence others. Forgiving also allows me to get quality rest at night. I strongly recommend it.

I recall my most impactful moment of forgiveness that set me on a path for success. It was asking forgiveness from someone that I knew would never respond: my father. I truly felt that we grew closer when I moved to Chicago and lived the life of a gangster and drug dealer. We spoke much more often compared to when I was growing up. Once he passed and I moved down to Florida, I started going to therapy. My sessions identified some areas where my dad was lacking. In my heart, I held it against him. I needed to forgive my dad, "But how could I? He was dead."

My therapist helped me understand that my dad could only support me so much because of his basic education and the culture in Jamaica for men. So, after therapy, I carried on my life, seeking growth and change. As we continued to unpack my journey in our sessions, I used to consistently ask my dad why he didn't share these things with me. I felt like I got nothing from him. As a grown adult, I was still yearning for that fatherly love. While at the therapist's office, I understood he could have only shared with me what he knew, which was very little.

One evening, I was in my kitchen about to cook dinner, and in my spirit, I was propelled to ask my dad for forgiveness. I wanted to let go of holding him responsible for the things I have learned, and the resentment I had for him. It became puzzling because I was taught you ask for forgiveness, and someone forgives you. I was reminded of a story from the Bible when Jesus was on the cross. A thief approached Jesus and ask for Jesus to remember him when he gets to his kingdom. The response given was, "Today, you will be with me in paradise."

Forgiveness frees one soul and mind. It allows you to engage in your passion and seize opportunities that God has in store for you. After this reflection, I asked my dad for forgiveness. I cried like a baby on the kitchen floor for about 20 minutes. That was one of the best feelings I have felt ever since. If I can ask a dead person for forgiveness and not seek a response, I can do the same for you who is alive and moving towards greatness.

♦ ♦ ♦

For me, letting go of the old and implementing the new Pete was critical on my leadership journey. This realization may happen in different ways for each individual, but the most important thing was inspecting what I expected. If I expected to have healthy relationships, I needed to start being a man of my word and get comfortable with uncomfortable conversations. If I expected to be an effective leader, I needed to start acquiring and implementing the skills of an effective leader. Now, just like any change, this does not happen overnight and requires you to invest time into yourself. This is when you PRACTICE! PRACTICE! PRACTICE! Get comfortable and familiar with your craft or passion.

By this time, I have corrected 20+ years of bad behaviors, which does not change overnight. Having Michael, my accountability partner, was critical to my process. Having an accountability partner will improve your growth as well once you find that individual. Michael kept me motivated and held me accountable for my actions, whereabouts, and words.

Many of us already have this individual in our lives and conduct these behaviors, but they are not strategic and intentional. For example, we already do this by having best friends. Best friends are meant to be honest with us and always look out for our best interests, no matter the cost. Because our best friends sometimes are at our level, they cannot get us to where we want to go. But these behaviors are already there. All you need to do is seek similar characteristics from someone at the level you desire to aspire towards. The accountability partner's experience can be a source of support for us, mentally and emotionally.

How does one find this accountability partner? This has been the struggle for many leaders based on discussions and surveys I have conducted. Leaders do not know where to start or know what to look for in an accountability partner. I have a process to identify this person using the MUST-SHOULD-COULD methodology.

One can break these three categories down into columns and prioritize them with bullet points. This list took me some time to create. Remember, this person will have a direct impact on your development and success. Do not rush the process but trust the process!

Your first column, the MUST column, will include the characters your accountability partner MUST come with. For example, I needed someone who had a story of success through hard work. The MUST column can be considered the areas in your life where you are weak and need the utmost development. I wanted to know how to view and handle my finances both personally and professionally. For me, that was also in my MUST column. I listed that the individual MUST earn an income of $250,000 a year while having a heart and gives back to the community.

The SHOULD column is characteristics that can be supported by someone else if your accountability partner is not strong in that area. For example, I listed in my SHOULD column that my accountability partner does not have to be a lover of sports. The reason for this was because I was a lover of soccer and was already a part of many soccer groups. That area in my life didn't need development. I was not seeking to become a professional soccer player. But it would be great if my accountability partner was a soccer player. That way, we could further connect.

The final column, your COULD column, can be difficult to complete at times. This is the area in your life that needs little development. It can be considered your strength column: the things you are already great at. I knew my passion for teaching, coaching, training, and speaking was being developed by John Maxwell and his team. So, in my COULD column, I listed that the accountability partner did not have to be a speaker.

My journey may be a bit different than yours because I had the John Maxwell team working on a specific area in my life. You may need that accountability partner to have the same passion you desire. However, do not compromise your list to locate the right accountability partner. Keep in mind, I did not say when you have found the perfect accountability partner. I want you to understand this person is human and not perfect. They may make mistakes while being your accountability partner.

You can and will surely find the right person based on your MUST-SHOULD-COULD list. They will assist you in connecting with the right people who can support your passion more effectively. When implemented, this approach is proven to provide positive results for me and those I coach. Discover your process, build and trust it, and watch your new life unfold. You will feel fulfilled every day of your life moving forward.

Now that we have identified your accountability partner, we can create your vision board and work towards accomplishing each task. Remember to celebrate each accomplishment along the way. Your accountability partner will be there to guide and support you. Do not be afraid to make mistakes but remember to correct them. There may be times where you and your accountability partner may see things differently. Do not take things personally and trust the process. Focus on your strength and connect with those who possess the skills in the areas you are weak in. Aim to expand your knowledge but collaborate for quality delivery and success.

I remember once, I wanted to reprimand one of my training assistants for not getting something done. It was impacting our performance drastically. I was going to act out of emotion and without facts. But after speaking with Michael, he instructed me to research further and communicate more. I should inspect what I expected before jumping to conclusions. Later, I discovered it was a typed error, which was done at the executive level, which was then corrected. Trusting the process saved my leadership credibility at that moment. But it also was a huge learning point. It is a fond memory recorded in the treasures of my leadership experiences. As you move forward, embrace your change, and share your growth and development with family and friends.

♦ ♦ ♦

I started working at a call center and was trying to learn as much as I could. I wanted to be a good worker. This goal was based on the principles that my mother had taught me as a child. It always goes back to childhood teachings as Dr. Bruce Lipton stated. The first seven years of a child's life are crucial to their adulthood and the type of man or woman they become. I started to meet new people and created new friendships. This was an opportunity to work on the new Pete. I rarely shared with people my past life because I did not want to be judged or treated differently. So, I kept my past life a secret for a long time.

At work, we had teams. There was a young man I spoke to quite often because he was friendly. He was also from Jamaica, and he would try to date as many women as possible. In Jamaica, we would say 'him look every woman wey pass him.' This was Charles.

There was a girl on our team named Diana. Just by looking at her, I knew that she came from a good home and was a Christian. Knowing Charles' intentions, I decided mentally that I would not allow him to talk to her. He had a level of respect for me based on how I dealt with him. He knew I was intelligent but also street smart. So, he listened to everything I said or told him to do. Again, leadership is influence, and I have had these traits in me for a long time, they just needed to be developed, and I needed guidance.

One day as we were heading to lunch, we passed Diana. I had decided mentally that I would protect her from my friend. Without his knowledge of my mental protection, on our way to lunch, Charles stopped and tried to talk to her. I immediately stepped in and said, "Yo that's my wife."

Before I could finish my statement, he said, "Alright mi boss; my bad I didn't know. No disrespect!"

I responded, "Ok, do not let it happen again."

Ever since then, Charles never said another word to her. All this time, I had yet to speak with this young lady. I only knew her name because we were on the same team.

Whenever Charles and I would see her, he would say, "Pete, there's your wife.

And I would say, "Yeah."

This went on for weeks, and I had yet to speak with Diana.

Around Thanksgiving time, my team at work had planned to host a potluck. This is where everyone on the team would bring a dish, and we would have lunch together. It was a form of team-building activity, and we enjoyed it. I decided to cook callaloo and saltfish as my contribution to the potluck.

At lunchtime, we were all in the break room eating. Diana was sitting at a table eating by herself, and I decided to join her. She had a beautiful smile and seemed so soft and tender. I was a guy coming from a rough life and was more familiar with an outspoken female with a little spice and aggression. She was different, and she spoke soft and proper. I was impressed.

After lunch, I asked her out on a date. She rejected because she was going to attend a youth convention that weekend. But then she stated we could go out when she returned. As we continued to speak, I confirmed she was a Christian and actively involved in her church. Although I was changing, my mentality towards relationships did not change. I was solely focused on my personal and professional development and image.

Diana returned from the youth convention, and we went out on a few dates. I met her mom, and then I was invited to church. When I started this job, I still had the dreadlock hairstyle and asked her if it was a problem, knowing she was a Christian. Her response was no. So, at times I would make a joke and sing to her a song written by one of Bob Marley's sons how she fell in love with a Rastaman. It was while at this job, trying to find a better job, I experienced discrimination because of dreadlock hairstyle and decided to cut it. Her parents were amazing, and we had a great relationship, which helped our relationship as we dated. I began attending church with her on Sundays and was introduced as her boyfriend. In collaboration with her parents, I proposed to her on Valentine's Day at a dinner hosted at the church. I had moved on to another job-seeking growth, development, and better pay. I was now seeking to start my own family. A few months later, we got married.

Activity

MUST-SHOULD-COULD Exercise!
- Specific to this chapter:
- If Single: Life partner sheet
- If Relationship: Renewal Sheet (Our relationship MUST-SHOULD-COULD)

Both: New life sheet (My new life MUST-SHOULD-COULD)

Chapter 7

Team Together, Team Apart

(The Struggle of New Beginnings)

Now I was settled in South Florida with a wife. I moved out of my mom's home and moved in with Diana and her parents. Every Sunday after church, we would have dinner together as a family. On birthdays and anniversaries, we committed to celebrate with each other and would go out to a restaurant together. I became a member of the church and started to get involved with the ministry. I attended the men's ministry and other church events. Diana was a part of the finance team, which required her to stay after church to organize the funds collected.

Eventually, we purchased a home and moved in together. She got a job with one of the cities within our county. She worked her way up from a contractor to a permanent employee. While for me, I was growing at my new job. I was promoted from customer service representative I (CSR I) to customer service representative II (CSR II).

I started to meet new people and create new relationships as I learned and understood the Christian faith. I was working on the new Pete. I strived to be consistent in my personal and professional behavior. My focus was to find the new Pete and develop him while other areas of my life, like intimacy, were put to the side.

As time passed, I became more active in the church and took on roles such as youth director and board member of the men's ministry. Those days were super fun, and I learned a lot wearing those leadership hats. Some of the fun times were movie nights, skating, and, most importantly, our prayer evenings at the altar. Surprisingly, I believed that the youths learned more when we took them outside the church. We taught them how to apply Godliness to everyday life.

Annually, I started to attend the same youth convention my wife attended the first time she rejected my invitation on a date.

I continued to grow professionally and was promoted from CSR II to Training Assistant within the training department. In this role, I discovered my passion to teach, coach, train, and speak the company process within the training department. It felt as if I was a newborn baby in the classroom every time I stood up to teach. I loved being interactive and at the front of the classroom because I felt great doing it. Lives were impacted whenever I did it. I saw how much I invested in my passion. I wanted to be the best. I felt empowered to inspire others through training and development, but I still lacked effective leadership. However, all this time, the behavior of having multiple women was never addressed and resolved.

Under the leadership of Bishop Lyttle Jr. I became a deacon, and head of the ushering department. I still maintained the role of youth director and board member of the men's ministry. At that time, I held a total of five leadership roles on top of my job. But it did not end there; I later became one of the Armor Bearers to the new pastor. Armor Bearers are the right-hand men to the pastor. It was a total of three young men and our wives who were each Armor Bearers to the First Lady, Bishop Lyttle's wife. This was one of the most privileged roles I have held as a leader, especially to be handpicked to support the pastor.

This was the first time out of the classroom I felt truly empowered. Regardless of whether you were inside or outside the organization, if you need to speak to the pastor, send him a message, or invite him to speak, an individual would speak to one of the Armor Bearers first. We spent a lot of quality time with the pastor as he traveled as a guest speaker visiting different churches. In those moments, we had the manly talk. It was different, nonviolent, and done with love compared to what I was familiar with on the street corners of Jamaica and in Chicago. With this access, I observed and learned the operations of a church, what an experience. Thank you, bishop!

He introduced me to John Maxwell through a leadership program he delivered to a few of us. This was with the intent for us to grow. John Maxwell and his team helped take me to the next level of leadership. Another promotion! This time I moved from Training Assistant to Trainer. I was now responsible for my own class and the material being delivered to each new employee who was under my leadership. My goal was always to graduate 100% to the production floor, or to keep attrition low. This now confirmed my passion for teaching, speaking, and inspiring others. I felt like I was in heaven every time I taught or spoke to a group of people or an individual.

I started to dig deeper into this gift as I shared my passion with my new bishop. I would observe him and other bishops whenever he traveled as a guest speaker. This is what I wanted to become. Having a first-row seat and access was priceless. This exposure to ministry had surely opened up my eyes to things I never knew happened inside a church. The diversity in behaviors and issues that people within the church wanted to resolve with the bishop was surprising and shocking. The overall operation of a church was informative and interesting.

♦ ♦ ♦

The word got out as I consistently produced quality CSR being transitioned to the production floor from training. I read surveys and reviews about my passion and the work I invested in teaching, training, coaching, and speaking. They were impressive. I continued to discover a little more about who I am and how I operated. The one thing was for sure: I influenced those around me to do, whatever it may be. People of both sexes were attracted to me. I became popular at work as almost every new employee who worked at our site was trained while I worked in the department.

I was in that role for a little over three years. But how do I handle all this attention? Attention from females flirting and wanting an affair with me. This was similar to the gang but in the corporate world. Still I had no effective leadership to emulate, so I did what I knew best. I took advantage when possible. I slept with as many girls as I could while leading in all these capacities, from the gang to the cooperate world, to church. There were few men in the church who opened up and shared their stories, so I hid my dirty behaviors.

One of the greatest attributes of leadership is sharing one's vision and being available to connect with those you lead. For example, if your manager at work was never there to support or guide you, one would say the manager is not effective—the same within a household. However, my culture promotes having multiple children in different households. I ask my Jamaican men: how do you lead in the homes you are not present? Children learn from their eyes. A phone call or a visit cannot help a child grow. I encourage us, men, to build your kingdom and lead under one household. Vision is important and needs to be shared. It allows those you lead to know how they play an essential role in accomplishing the vision.

A leader's actions and words should support the shared vision. This means that leaders must communicate on a regular basis the progress towards the vision. Leaders must use their strength to engage those you lead. I learned early in my leadership journey that you need to focus on meeting the needs of those you lead. Naturally, in return, they will meet and, in most cases, exceed your needs. To lead people, you must love people at home and work.

I recommend you write your goals down and share them with your accountability partner for support and guidance. For 90% of the goals I have set, I try to find some portrait of the idea and print it. Then hang it in my home as a daily reminder. This method is critical to my process and has been successful on my leadership journey. Be precise and clear in your goals.

In talking with many persons I have met, I discovered they are afraid of sharing their vision or passion for the following reasons. They do not prepare ahead of time to talk about their vision and passion with others. Due to a lack of preparation, they do not sound confident when responding. Then they do not think they are qualified enough for others to buy into their vision. Maybe because of a lack of finance, they think it is not even worth mentioning. They think that no one will invest in them!

I learned quickly and early in my leadership journey that one must sell themselves like it is a sales job. It was important for my process to see my passion as a sell. I had to sell myself as a leader. After having such a bad experience in Chicago selling alarm systems door-to-door, I never thought I would positively view sales. I recall that in one of my prior jobs, I had completed training and started working on the operation floor. A few coworkers had approached me on different occasions to talk about my dress code. They felt since I was out of training and passed probation, I could stop wearing my dress pants and a buttoned-down shirt. A year later, the vice president sent out a company-wide notice of a change in our dress code, similar to what I had been wearing every day. I was blamed for the change by a few coworkers.

In leadership, developing oneself has a direct impact on those we lead. As parents, we should remain consistent. I shared with those I worked with that I wanted to be a part of the executive team. I did not see any of those individuals dress like what I saw at my site. So, I dressed for what I wanted to become. And guess what, I got promoted to a role which was stationed in the executive building. I was one step closer to becoming a part of the executive team.

If you are that leader seeking support and development, ask yourself this question: Why am I doing the things I am doing? There should be a purpose behind what you do. This is where your vision lives. Write things down and watch your vision come to life. My vision is to provide knowledge and resources to others to allow them to live a fulfilled life daily. What is your vision?

Therefore, having an accountability partner is important to everyone. This person would be able to support, teach, and guide you through these new experiences with testimonies to share. One can make decisions that impact them negatively, which impacts all areas of their life. An accountability partner can prevent bad decisions.

In my life, I shared with Michael my struggles on having affairs with multiple women at once. This is a conversation Michael and I discuss consistently. I share events and experiences to ensure I remain focused, and my behaviors are aligned with my passion and vision. Over time, due to the regular conversations with

Michael, the new behaviors became a part of my subconscious mind. I started to turn away women seeking to develop an intimate relationship with me. These conversations with Michael were not easy and comfortable in the beginning. But, over time, they became more comfortable.

With all the changes in my life, people were now asking me to be their accountability partner. This is an honor. It is similar to having a role model. This is teamwork, and your accountability partner should be doing their part as well. I strongly recommend you set expectations between yourself and your accountability partner to ensure all guidelines are agreed upon.

One time, before I went to a party, I shared with Michael that I was going out with some friends from my soccer group. To my surprise, while at the party, Michael showed up. We met through a mutual friend. This was done on a few occasions at different events. Later, I discovered Michael was building his trust and ensuring that I was a man of my word and nothing less.

Further into the relationship, this style was not needed anymore as I became a man of my word. Over time you should feel the support and love from your accountability partner as you journey along this path. However, your accountability partner is not your therapist or coach. They should become your confidant and close friend. Using the MUST-SHOULD-COULD worksheet, and with some homework on your part, you will find the right accountability partner. Next, I discovered this person will become a lifetime friend and confidant. Do not be surprised as you develop: the roles may change. Be humble and serve in the manner you have been served. This will be better for the individual.

I believe that life is not balanced and will never be. As we journey through life, different priorities take place as we strive to accomplish our goals and dreams. Therefore, it is critical to have effective communication in our relationships. That way our partners can support us. With this approach, we can work together to achieve individual goals. I believe in Team Together, Team Apart at home and work. This means that, with effective teamwork and communication within a team, everyone can become successful and achieve their individual goals.

My favorite sport, soccer, has 11 players on the field at any given time. Each player has a specific role. But during the game, if a player is out of position, one of his teammates can cover for him. With individual roles, each one of us has a specific place in the field. For example, I played defense and as a defender. My area of the field was in the back. But I can support or cover for a teammate out of position in midfield. A defender will move to the front of the field only when there is a set play like a free kick or a corner. Now, as a defender, I cannot win the game by myself. I need my forwards and midfielders to assist us. This is how we become a team together while being respectively responsible for our individual roles.

In soccer, there is constant communication during the game. This begins from the back of the field, with the goalkeeper and defenders having a vision of the entire pitch. Since I was introduced to leadership in high school through soccer, my talkative manner developed as I played the sport. The position I played on the field was defensive midfield or defensive, which required the player to talk a lot. And now, later in life, I became a teacher, trainer, coach, and speaker. I applied this process to my leadership journey and shared the vision and created a strategic plan to achieve the desired results.

I understand that you need a team to accomplish the big goals. I also know how essential my individual role works in achieving the goal or vision. This is team apart. Here you will see leadership qualities working hand-in-hand.

I recommend you analyze your youth. I believe your passion lives there. Leaders, you must share your vision and passion. That way, you can coach and develop. You must inspect what you expect, support, and guide. To lead people, you must love people!

Now I am comfortable, and my focus is on my family and building a strong marriage with my wife of a year. I later discovered my wife and I are two separate behavior profile types. I am an entertainer, and she was a thinker. In other words, I am an extrovert, and she is an introvert. I have a high sex drive, and she had a low sex drive. Now, why did not I find this out before marriage? Because my focus was on finding the new Pete, not sex. Diana assisted me with that process, but there were questions I should have asked before we got married. I did not ask because the focus was on change, which she brought to the table. And because I did not have my MUST-SHOULD-COULD worksheet, there were many things that were not discussed. We did not talk about growth, finance, and sex. These were my languages!

When I got settled in our marriage and I felt I had changed. My high intimacy was activated. Diana and I decided not to have sex before marriage. We were young, and we wanted to do the right thing. After marriage, it was still not a focus because I was embracing and enjoying the new Pete. I was focused on money. But in that marriage, I had covered up those old behaviors rather than addressing them. So, when I felt Diana was not meeting my sexual needs, I went to other women. It was simple because I attracted them easily. The cheating began all over again.

I knew no other way to handle the issue. I was not yet comfortable with uncomfortable conversations. I found refuge in those other women and would tell them what they wanted to hear to sleep with them. This was while I was still active in five leadership roles between work and church. I was effective as a leader and helping others to perform at their best, personally and professionally. While personally, I was failing.

At home, I was quiet, just like my father. I would communicate, address, and resolve issues at work. But when I got home, our issues lingered for months. I ignored numerous attempts by Diana to resolve them. Due to this lack of leadership, my marriage turned for the worst. I stopped sleeping in our bed, and we lived like roommates. We drove separate cars to church; although, we would leave around the same time from the house. For the first 18 years of my life, I witnessed and observed shying away from uncomfortable conversations. When confronted, I would witness the men attempt to turn the situation into something violent. I was not going to abuse Diana physically, which means my next option was to shy away from the issue.

However, I was not shying away at work. I was performing at a high level and was nominated for the Peak award—winning a trip to Maui, Hawaii, for two. On top of that, I was in the 10% of top performers nationwide. So, I was awarded a trip to Hollywood, California, for two. On both trips Diana accompanied me. It was on those trips that I truly observed our differences. I wanted to have sex most of the time, and she did not. I wanted to go out and see the town, but she preferred to sleep. We argued during most of both trips.

A few months later, I was selected to present one of our site's internal TV commercials that described leadership and success. Again, this exposure came with more attention from all types of women. The stories I heard on the street corners of Jamaica growing up was right in front of me with easy access. Is this what God had ordained for me? I know it was not, but how I was raised had influenced me. I slept with as many women as possible without them knowing about the others.

Once after sleeping with a young lady, I saw horns on her head like the devil in my spirit. I quickly left because I knew that this is not where I should be.

I felt horrible and asked myself, "Pete, what did you gain from that?"

Shortly after, we had a guest speaker at church who was a prophetic woman. When she had made her altar call, as leaders we went forth to assist anyone coming to the altar. She later spoke to me and said that I would become wealthy one day and travel the world because I influenced others. She said this for the entire church to hear.

But then she whispered in my ear, "Do not lay your head in the lap of any Jezebel."

What did this mean? At the time, I had no clue.

Activity

Accountability Worksheet

Chapter 8

Strengthening the Arm

(Therapy...the Best Decision Ever)

My leadership journey continued as I transitioned from the customer service industry to banking. I was consistently performing at a high level, and my district manager assigned me to every branch in the Northwest district. This plan was with the intent that I would improve the branch and move on.

It surely worked. Each branch I was assigned to, our customer service surveys increased as well as employee performance. This was good for the employee and the branch. I was now assigned to a branch that was only seven minutes away from home. This was great as I could go home for lunch as well as sleep longer because it was so close. Our house was also about 20 minutes away from my mother.

One day, I decided to go home for lunch. When I got there, I saw a U-Haul truck in my driveway. There were no other cars, so I thought that maybe my neighbor was using my driveway while I was not home. As I walked towards my front door, I looked back at the U-Haul truck and noticed the back of the truck was open as well as my front door.

At first, I immediately thought I was being burglarized. In panic and shock, I ran to the back door where I was able to see inside my home. I pressed myself against the glass door, which had no curtain. I saw two men coming down the stairs with my bed, but to my amusement, they were not acting like thieves. Now further confused, I hastily rushed back to the front and entered the house to inquire what was happening.

After speaking with the movers, they explained that Diana hired them to move her into her new apartment. In total shock and dismay, Diana was moving out of our home without my knowledge. I quickly ran up the stairs and found her packing up her items. She explained she was tired of my cheating ways and had to leave. If I had not gone home for lunch, after work, I would have walked into a nearly empty home.

Speechless, sweating, and heart pounding, I looked in the mirror and told myself something must change. God did not create us to walk imbalanced, so my life should not be imbalanced. Professionally, everything was great. I saw growth and a new Pete. But personally, my intimate relationships were the same. At that moment, I decided to seek therapy. It was **the best decision ever!** I returned to work numb and confused, but, luckily, the end of our shift was near. I returned home that evening to an empty bedroom and half of a living room set.

I was now living alone and felt disappointed and sad. No one knew of our separation. Months passed, so it was time to alert my mother and my bishop of our situation. Both were shocked and disappointed. Then both of them encouraged me to strive for better. They knew I had more to offer. Additionally, they both supported me in going to therapy. I was demoted from my leadership roles in the ministry. However, no one at work knew because I kept wearing my wedding ring.

The lifestyle of having multiple women was the only life I knew. So, after my Diana had moved out, it continued. I kept having affairs with multiple women. Months later, Diana filed for a divorce. I constantly hid from the officer who tried to summon me with those court papers.

One night, I was prepping dinner. I looked out of the kitchen window, which faced our driveway. I saw the officer pulling into my driveway, and I never answered the door when he knocked. Another evening, I was taking my groceries out the trunk of my car.

The officer walked up, and without any notice, he said, "Mr. Kennedy, you are being served."

Then he handed me the divorce court documents. I felt disappointed and sad again. Deep down inside, I did not want a divorce. But I continued to have multiple affairs, even though I was not emotionally attached to any of them.

I started therapy immediately after having sex with a young lady who I thought had horns on her head. I quickly stopped our activity and went home. The next day, I searched for a therapist within my company resources. I started my first therapy session the following week. When I saw the horns on that young lady, I knew it was God showing me a sign. It was time for me to stop and be a better man, husband, and friend. I chose to be obedient to my spirit. Therapy, here I come. The only person who knew of my lifestyle to that extreme was Kizzy, and he did not live near me.

All my sessions were scheduled for 8 AM, right before work. My therapist was short and reminded me of my grandmother. She had a sturdy body for a woman. However, she was soft-spoken. She was short, and her legs would hang whenever she sat in her chair. Her name was Sarah, and she had been in practice for over ten years.

In therapy, I discovered my entertainer style, which is a person who enjoys people. With this style, I can influence others. I am a leader, father, husband, friend, brother, cousin, uncle, and business associate. I understand how to communicate and enrich relationships for the better. My aha moment in therapy was understanding who I attract and their behaviors. This is what I did not understand in the past.

I believe that one needs a therapist to identify their issues and a coach to help develop the passion. I learned there were two types of people I attract: one that admires me and others who are admirable of me. My therapist broke it down for me. She said there are people who admire me and want to see me be successful and achieve the best. On the other hand, there are people who are admirable of me and want a piece of my success. Wow! What a discovery! I felt a weight falling off me when I identified this about myself and those I interact with.

Melanie and Crystal admired me, while Susan was admirable of me. Believe me, going forward, I could identify these women within 15-minutes of interacting with them. Identifying these behaviors was my turning point, and this book is an attempt to avoid others from living a similar lifestyle. Or if you are still living this lifestyle, how you can make a change for the better no matter where you are in life.

During my sessions, it was also confirmed that I am a great leader, and I truly care about the success of others. My passion to speak and influence others has been a part of me since childhood, but no one took the time to identify and develop these skills. During all of this, I would often talk to my bishop about leadership. One day, he introduced me to John Maxwell, where I started to study more about leadership.

Once my therapy sessions with Sarah were completed, and we had identified the problem, it was now time to correct and enhance myself. I believe therapy is the identification process. From there, we need a coach for the development process. I was blessed to be connected with the John Maxwell leadership team. It was right up my alley – just perfect. The book we studied was *Developing the Leader Within You* by John Maxwell. I remember this quote from the book that has never left me.

"Not all change is improvement – but without change, there can be no improvement."

When I read this quote from John, I realized that change is what I needed to improve myself. These changes can be small, but I need to at least start moving the needle.

♦ ♦ ♦

I still had an arm, so all I needed to do was follow through with therapy for proper healing and strength. Well, I did not follow through with therapy for my hand, which was another mistake I made. If I had attended therapy, that would have allowed me to improve my left hand's functionality. But because I did not make good decisions, I still cannot hold a plate of food with full strength. My left hand is weak and begins to shake and itch. It is not 100% healed properly. Therapy was needed!

Since I made such a mistake with me healing my body, I decided I was not going to make a similar mistake mentally on my leadership journey. Leaders must develop their strengths. What is your strength? There are many things we do well, but I consider a leader's strength is embedded in their passion. To develop this strength as a leader or parent, you must know who you are, and the behavior profiles associated with the characters that define you. When you discover who you are, you can also identify your purpose in life.

I mentioned in chapter 1 the four behavior styles I speak on when invited for keynote speaking or workshops.

They are:
1. Thinker
2. Entertainer
3. Controller
4. Feeler

There are many tools available to identify your behavior profile. Please invest in knowing who you are. It will be critical to your success as a leader and parent. Everyone's passion provides an opportunity for us as leaders and parents to serve. Giving back to our communities with our talents and gifts to those less fortunate should be to inspire, support, and guide them to similar success.

Once, as a youth director, there was a youth that I began to personally mentor. His name was Bryan. I discovered after visiting his home one day, that everything I tried to teach into the Bryan's life was positive. But at home, his mom did everything opposite. When I would drive home, I understood why it was difficult for Bryan to remain consistent with the things we were trying together. His mom was not on board with the changes.

I didn't want to lose Bryan, so I decided that I needed his mom to know who I was and my intentions for her son. So I visited them more often. After developing a relationship with Bryan's mom, I discovered she did not know how to support Bryan, which is why she rejected the change within Bryan. Years later, after remaining close friends with the family, I regularly checked in with the mom. Bryan transitioned to college and excelled. His mom continued to develop herself to this day by reading and going to workshops.

♦ ♦ ♦

When a man loves, that person develops themself to be strong in their beliefs and character. When this love is developed, an individual can offer 100% of themselves to whatever or whomever they desire to, personally and professionally. But this starts when one identifies who they are. You must love you first. Then you can love and share with others.

In sports, some of the world's greatest coaches are those who have played the game in the past. They can relate to their team because they have their own experiences and stories to share. This builds trust with the players and allows each player to follow the direction or guidance of the coach. The best players are consistently developing their craft at the game they love. Why are leaders any less?

Effective leaders consistently learn, grow, and enhance themselves for those they lead and interact with, personally and professionally. PRACTICE! PRACTICE! PRACTICE! One must make sound decisions based on their environment and what they desire for themselves. Observe your life and make decisions to better yourself. If going to therapy will make you a better person, do it for yourself.

Passion drives action, which turns into servitude. When this change takes place and is accepted by a leader, we automatically become community servants. At this stage in your leadership journey, I strongly recommend that if you can connect with inner-city schools, you should help our youths who are underprivileged. They are seeking a role model/accountability partner. Allowing them to get access to successful leaders like yourselves can help them to identify from early their passion. This gets them closer to living a fulfilled life.

There is a saying, "When you discover your passion, you never work another day in your life."

For myself, I live and breathe teaching, training, coaching, and speaking every day. In the early stages of my leadership journey, accepting and developing my behavior profile was not easy. Including my family and friends was a tremendous help to adapt my passion and implementing the behaviors in daily life.

♦ ♦ ♦

I remember assisting a family member with online activities, like airline ticket purchases, emails, etc. due to them living in another state. We had a family event to attend, and the family member came to stay with us and asked for my assistance like they normally would. I took the opportunity to teach the family member since we were in each other's presence. I showed them how to do all the things I would help with when we are apart. It went well! This was a change for me and those involved in my life.

Every decision we make as leaders has an impact, whether they are positive or negative on those around us. Through my lens, I want to encourage leaders and parents to start something. Make a move. Observe and ask questions about the traditions that are in place. Review and study whether these traditions will set you up for success. If they do not set you up for success, seek a different approach to ensure you can live a fulfilled life while being a servant to others.

I strongly recommend therapy for everyone. Then after therapy, you need a coach. The John Maxwell leadership team helped tremendously. This is where I believe many leaders make a mistake: they seek coaching from a therapist. A therapist's job is to help you identify the issue, while a coach helps you to enhance your passion.

Therapy truly helps, but one must be honest and open with their therapist. Therapy was the best decision I have made as a man because it allowed me to understand where I was going wrong in my relationships. This was my biggest personal downfall.

In my culture, whenever I mention therapy to anyone, the first response is, "Nutten nuh wrong wid me (nothing is wrong with me)."

Seeking a therapist does not mean something wrong is with you. It does not mean you are insane or psychopathic. It allows one to identify their true selves and find ways how to improve on those identified behaviors.

Throughout my childhood, my mother had nicknamed my dad 'Promise'. All because he would promise to take me to the countryside with him and never did. After going through therapy, I discovered I held on to a lot of things my father never did for me, and I had resentment towards him in my heart. I used to wonder, why didn't my dad talk to me about these things? I was his son.

Now, my mother also did not realize the impact that this nickname would have on me later in life, or else she would not have done it. I witnessed the same behavior on the street corners where men were not of their word. I became one of those men, especially in my marriage. And later, it failed. As parents, we must be careful of the names we use and the things we do for our children to see. My therapist helped me heal as I discovered that my dad could not pass on to me what he did not have. I need to forgive him and move on.

♦ ♦ ♦

The day I feared I had arrived. Diana and I were scheduled to appear in court on a Wednesday morning. We were in front of the judge together. He asked us questions about our relationship and our experiences. A half an hour later, I was divorced. My ex-wife and I remained in contact as we did not hate each other. She was just fed up with my behavior and wanted out. This destroyed me because this was not what I desired for our marriage. Even after the judge had finalized our divorce, I was emotionally wrecked.

I did constant research on how I could cope with this divorce. I discovered a type of therapy called dissolution of marriage therapy. I asked my now ex-wife if she would go with me, even though it was just a few sessions. It was a tremendous help in healing my divorce process.

I strongly suggest this for couples who are separating and find it difficult to handle the breakup. I suggest you seek counseling together, not necessarily to restore the relationship, but how to handle the separation. You might be luckier than I was and restore your relationship. In turn, I knew how to be a better man for the next woman I would call my wife.

Activity

Part A: Hard Topic Fear
- Return to Chapter 5 and refresh your mind on your hard topics.
- Read through the things you're afraid of hearing.
- Pick one.
- Imagine that a therapist has pinpointed it as your problem.

Part B: Seek Action
- Research online coaches on the life area of your "problem".
- From initial results, write down 3 Coaches.

_____

_____

_____

Part C: Purpose Alignment
- Write down your purpose from Chapter 3:

  _____

- Further Research: Now that you have the names of coaches, go further into their information. Read their MISSION Statements.
- How does Option 1 align with your purpose?: _____

  _____

- Option 2? _____

  _____

- Option 3? _____

  _____

BONUS: Make an appointment
- If they're offering any form of consultation, follow through on your Hard Topic conversation.
- 1-on-1 offerings
- Webinars with Q & A

Chapter 9

Sharing Renewal
(And a Major Loss Within the Research)

I felt like a newborn baby. After participating in two truly helpful therapy sessions, I was ready to enhance myself to the next level. I decided to develop my passion for teach, train, coach, and speak. Additionally, I started to study more of John Maxwell's book.

I remember as a child in church, a Bible story that was referenced said that a man should love his wife the way God loves the church. I chose to interpret that for all love, specifically on sincere brotherly love. I wanted to understand why we weren't physically or verbally affectionate with each other. Along the journey of my leadership studies and development, I began to research my culture and how our men lead and love.

I have heard it said that in Jamaica during slavery, bucking was used whenever a male slave would rebel against his slave master or seen as a leader amongst the slaves. The slave master would tie the male slave up in front of the entire plantation and rape him for all to see. Due to this act, the male slaves in Jamaica have resentment towards homosexuality, which has since been internalized through the Jamaican culture and generations of men on the island. Imagine being a child who has been raised by a man and never heard the words "I love you" from that male figure. Think about how it feels to never be hugged and loved by a father figure or male role model. Well I can tell you, it feels horrible and makes you feel as if you are not loved and valued by your parents or role model. The Bible says the people shall perish due to lack of knowledge. I can say I have made some mistakes due to the lack of knowledge of who I am.

♦ ♦ ♦

As a trainer, I was offered a leadership role to travel and be exposed to different time zones in America. Our site was ranked #1, and I was a part of those top performers. These results offered more opportunities to travel. These trips were to aid in launching other customer service sites and support other sites with leadership development.

What I didn't anticipate was that one of these trips would change my views on how a man loves. Our company was launching a site in Iloilo, Manila, and Pampanga, Philippines. They asked a few trainers from our site if we, our company trainers, could travel to assist with the launch. These launches would include training the entire leadership staff and new employees on the company's policies and procedures. This trip to the Philippines was scheduled for three to six months. Our final month was to observe and modify when needed.

I had to get shots from a medical doctor to travel and a few other items before leaving the US. I was excited to see this side of the world. I arrived in Manila the first night then flew to Iloilo the following day. I was shocked to see how similar Jamaica was to the Philippines. I could see parts of downtown Kingston in Manila. It was a huge dirty city with bus engine sounds passing along each side of the small two-lane road with black smoke coming from the exhaust. The bus was packed with passengers from front to back. These buses reminded me of Jamaica. Small motorcycles would slip through traffic as they tooted their bike horns. I was amazed and could not wait to see the rest of the Philippines.

But two experiences had a major impact on my life forever.

The first was when I was teaching. One of my styles as a trainer was to walk around the classroom as I taught. I noticed one day in class, as I walked the room, there was a student that would shy away from me whenever I got close. I did not think anything of it; different cultures, a different style, maybe. But it continued every time I would walk the room. Then I became curious because he was the only one reacting this way. He was short with a bald head and wore glasses. This guy was about ten years older than me and did not speak in class at all.

While in the States, we were instructed that this culture would be different, and we should focus on delivering the material. So, outside of teaching, I wanted to see the inner cities of Iloilo, especially because I was from the inner cities of Jamaica.

I developed a good relationship with the students in the class. One night, they invited me to one of their huts for an overnight cookout on the beach. I said yes, of course. We arrived at the hut, and, again, I felt as if I was back home in Jamaica. The huts were on the beach, like in Jamaica. My students and their families started to cook from a wood fire and kerosene pan as we do in Jamaica. They were running a boat. It's a Jamaican phrase for when a group of friends gather together and bring resources to cook, eat, talk, and spend quality time together. This is exactly what we were doing miles away in Iloilo, Philippines.

As dinner was being prepared, I listened to stories about hopes to leave Iloilo for better opportunities. They prepared a similar bird dish we eat in Jamaica. Balut was a baby duck in a shell sold and eaten on the streets on Iloilo. In Jamaica, we have brown stew chicken, and, in the Philippines, the same dish is called chicken adobo like so many other similarities to Jamaica. I felt at home.

Finally, it was time to eat. The food was shared, and everyone had to get their plate from the table in the middle. When I got my plate, I noticed there were no utensils. I asked and was told that utensils are only provided in restaurants. Otherwise, everyone else eats with their hands. This was new to me because we ate with utensils no matter when and where in Jamaica.

As I look around to find somewhere to sit and eat, there was an open spot next to the guy in class who always seemed shy whenever I walked the room. I was curious about his behavior and saw this as an opportunity to connect with him, so I sat beside him. He reacted the same way as usual in class, head bowed, shoulders tucked in, and his eyes were closed. He was sending me a message that he didn't want to connect. With boldness, I asked him if everything was ok? His answer changed my life.

He said, "Pete, I enjoy your class and look forward to coming to work every day, but at this stage in my life, I never knew I would ever meet a black man."

I almost fell off the seat. In shock and amazement, I said, "What?"

He continued, "I do not see black people where I am from, and I do not go to the mall because I cannot afford it. The closest I have seen a black man was on the television."

He began to pinch me as if I was not a real person. I could not believe what God was allowing me to experience, especially in the 21st century. I was the first black man this Philippine man has met. Not many black men can say this. It made me feel special, with all the millions of black people in this world, I was the first one he'd met. That is amazing, and it inspired me more that this was what I was called to do. Teach, train, coach, speak and develop others.

That incident humbled me since I view life differently and strive to impact my community one household at a time. He and I became good friends after that outing. I wanted to ensure I left a great impression based on my race since I was the first one he had met.

My second life-changing moment was even bigger. My connection with my students became stronger after that outing. They saw me outside the classroom, and we learned that our backgrounds were similar. Next, they invited me to a night club. I got dressed and one of the students picked me up before we left.

After about an hour in the nightclub, everyone started to drink, dance, and have fun. I was standing to the side, observing my surroundings and their behavior. My students and I hadn't hung out in a night club before, so I wanted to see how they reacted after a few drinks. To my surprise, the DJ started playing some reggae music, and, oh my gosh, the dance floor was now crowded. They loved reggae music! As everyone gathered on the dance floor, the space got smaller. I was used to a packed dance floor like the ones I attended at the dancehall parties when I was young.

As I rocked side to side, dancing to my culture's music, one of the guys came up and started to dance with me. I immediately pushed him from in front of me because this was not the norm for me. My subconscious mind reacted instinctively. Men don't dance together in Jamaica or the US, so this was unusual behavior.

In response, this guy and his friends, who saw me push him, approached me angrily, ready to fight. Another classmate stepped in and calmed the situation down. He explained to them that I was new to this.

"Pete does not know our culture; he didn't mean it."

They later realized this was not the norm for me, and we apologized to each other. He went on to dance with one of his other male friends. I cannot tell another man where I'm from that

I love him, much less to dance with him, without him thinking I am gay.

I thought to myself that these people were crazy. But it got worse! When it was time for us to leave, on our way to the car, all the men held hands as they walked and sang. They were feeling nice from their drink of liquor and dancing all night. Some even hugged each other as they walked. Now, this was even stranger for me. I never saw men act in this manner, and they are not gay.

The following day in class, I took some time to learn more about their culture and how men reacted to love. This was all new to me. I learned the men in the Philippines are taught how to love each other and their wives. Their fathers, grandfathers, and sometimes great-grandfathers consistently hugged them and would tell them that they love them. They were poor in finances but rich in love and affection. With this practiced behavior, a man who is gay will respect and honor those who are not with how they communicate and express love.

As I heard this, I thought out loud, and I blurted out in class, "Why my Jamaican men can't love like this?"

That question led to this book being written. The Philippines was a humbling experience that I would not change for the world. It opened my eyes. As men, we can genuinely love another man with no homosexual thoughts or intentions. Because of this, I've always said if I could take the entire island of Jamaica to visit Iloilo, Philippines for two weeks. Our island would be so much better after we return.

Men, love your sons, fathers, brothers, and any other male figure in your circle with a sincere heart. Leadership is Love, Love is Leadership!

I returned to the States and continued to research on this topic of leadership and love. I wanted to share this with my Jamaican friends. I started slowly among my friends. Without them anticipating it, I would express love to them verbally. They would get defensive as expected because this is how we were raised. I would always take this opportunity to start the conversation on love. Why, as men, do we react the way we do? I would share my Philippines' experience with men expressing love.

I would consistently express my sincere brotherly love in words and actions. Eventually, my guy friends believed me and accepted my love. I am not saying they did not love me before, but as men in my culture, we do not tell each other we love you. Although deep inside they know that they are not gay, regardless, in our culture, it is not the norm to be affectionate. My mission is to change this behavior and mindset. If we do not love our men and express it, who will?

♦ ♦ ♦

I received a call from my mother like normal. But this time, we did not have a normal conversation. She shared that she was ill and diagnosed with cancer. Wow, I was not prepared for such news and did not know what to expect or what questions to ask. I just wanted to support and be there for my mother as much as I could. I took her to many doctor appointments and chemo treatments. I took advantage of all our time spent together because I didn't know what tomorrow may bring.

Knowing my passion, she took the time to share with me stories about her and my dad. She told me she knew my dad had other women but ignored it. And because of this, he could not provide 100% for this family and how I should strive to be different. These stories and moments meant a lot to me because they drew us closer.

And then she said it.

"Pete, you have been a leader since a child. Continue this work and watch your dreams come to pass. You are great at what you do. I have seen it and enjoyed it when I saw you. You go, my Stumps!"

I did everything for her during this time. I cooked and cleaned for her. I also helped her shower, which was the most embarrassing thing I could do as a male. I cannot recall seeing her naked before, and, wow, it was strange to do it as an adult. But when you love someone, all of that does not matter. She told me she enjoyed it. See, God was looking out for me and allowed me to learn and get the stories needed. They live with me today.

It was a blessing to be by her side through this entire process until she died. Rather than getting a phone call that she was gone, God allowed us to express love to each other the same way she loved everyone else her entire life. Before my mother died, she wrote her eulogy and paid for her own funeral. She told me that all I had to do was show up. What a mother, up to the moment of her death, she made sure all was well, and we had nothing to worry about. Rest in peace Mrs. Joyce. You are truly missed but cannot be forgotten. Your legacy lives on!

After the burial of my mother, I had traveled to Jamaica to handle some business relating to her. With my research on my mind, I wanted to conduct an activity and observe the reaction of local men. I contacted Simone, one of my first girlfriends, who I was still good friends with after all these years of living in different countries. I shared my story and my idea, and she agreed to help me with the activity.

For the activity, I would treat her with love and respect in public and observe the response of others. This would include things like opening the door for her and holding hands in public. Most importantly, there would be no sleepovers to avoid any sexual interaction. We would do this every day. I proved in public when a guy displays love and affection, some think he is weak, or something is wrong with him. Or what could that girl have done, why he is treating her that way. Rather than, this should be the norm for all women to be treated. With the guy making his statement proved to me many were looking and thinking the same they were just not as bold as he was to say it. The verbal confirmation was needed to help support evidence for this book.

I listened to music as I looked out the windows of the airplane on my way to Jamaica. I was excited about my activity. Just like we planned, I picked her up in the morning and dropped her off at night every day. The entire time I was there, she would accompany me to all my appointments and tours around the island.

During that time, people stared and whispered to each other as I held her hand when we walked around or when I placed her in the car. No one said anything outward to us. As my trip was coming to an end, I went to purchase some KFC to bring home. We stopped at Manor Park plaza in Constant Spring. No one had said anything as we held hands on the way back to the car. I placed her in the car, closed the door, and walked behind the car to enter the driver's side. Then I heard a loud shout!

"Yo sah! Yo sah!"

I looked to see who the person was calling, and it was a security guard from one of the stores in the plaza.

He waved at me, and shouted, "A gold she hav under har why yuh a treat a har so."

He laughed, then went back into his store. What the security guard was saying was along the lines of 'does Simone's private body part comes in gold, why I am treating her with all this outward love?' This showed how men from my culture find it difficult to express love in their relationships.

I entered the car and said, "Thank you, Jesus!"

Simone asked what had happened, and I shared with her what the security guard had said. She then shared with me that, during the activity, she felt weird and out of place at times. She even tried to pull her hand away when I held it. All because she was not used to her hand being held. I was aware of this and held her hand even tighter when it happened, and we laughed about it.

I stuck to the process, and when it seemed I was not getting anywhere, I got the results I desired. Those results were that Jamaican men do not support love being expressed openly and consider these actions as weak. I gathered my results and flew back to the US.

Traveling to the Philippines humbled me and changed my views on love. What also amused me was how happy the Philippine people were while being financially unstable. As a young man, I owned my own home and had two cars. Compared to an average Philippine living in Iloilo, I would be considered wealthy. This propelled me to share my story in an attempt to change young mens' mindsets through my passion.

♦ ♦ ♦

Losing my mother was very painful, but I thank God for the way he played it out on my leadership journey. Throughout this process, I truly understood the magnitude and power that lies within obedience. I recall a story from the Bible that says obedience is better than sacrifice. It truly is and carries a lot of blessings with it.

In chapters three and five, I shared how obedience will bless you in the future. I strongly believe it sets you up for success. Because of obedience, I acquired my bachelor's degree and later a master's degree. As I stuck to the process along my leadership journey, I discovered my passion and started my own business. I was obedient to my best friend Kizzy, who gave me the advice to forgive the guy who shot me and move on. Look where I am today because of obedience.

One of the habits that Mrs. Joyce taught me from an early age is the habit of writing things down. This became essential in my life. I can hear her saying, "Pete, nothing beats pen and paper."

I didn't know that years later, this habit would be critical to my success. This is one of the few legacies that Mrs. Joyce left with me. As parents and leaders, ask yourselves what legacy am I leaving behind for my children? Every time I lead, I am always rewarded when I hear the words, "Pete, I will never forget you, thank you for all you have shared with me."

Be careful of the picture frames you create. Some can destroy you while others build you. Those good picture frames will come from effective and good leaders that you surround yourself with. I remember reading in one of John's books, how everyone he leads, he considers a friend. I use this similar approach. When I meet someone for the first time, I believe in giving them a fair chance to enhance themselves. I give them 100% trust. Trust grows throughout the relationship to allow the person to grow. I met and sat with John a few times. I saw him refer to me as a friend sincerely. I felt it and believed it. I have seen the positive impact on those I lead by practicing this behavior sincerely.

Parents: communicate and trust your children. Lead from example and show them the things they can accomplish in life. This is your investment: help them to be a success in life. Trust the process.

What is that process? Whenever I teach, train, coach, and speak, I share the examples of life processes we commit to every day to survive. For example, when it comes to driving a car, there is a process involved. For an automatic vehicle, you cannot place the car in drive unless the car is turned on, so the first step in the process of driving is to start the vehicle. Then we can move on to other steps, depending on what you want to do as a driver. For example, one can turn on the AC or stereo to the vehicle.

As simple as this may seem, you cannot skip step one of the process at all. I apply the same to leadership, parenting, relationships, and success. There is a process involved, and in many cases, you cannot skip a step in the process to move forward. If the system you are involved with allows it, many times, it may fail, and we have to start all over again. Create your process and trust it. This is similar to your MUST-SHOULD-COULD worksheet. Consistently review and modify your process for growth and enhancement. Once you connect all the behaviors and processes, one can establish a powerful and effective culture. This will leave a legacy for others to admire.

Activity

- Passion Action
- Self
- Friends
- Family
- Community
- Broken relationships
- Self-Action
- Write down something you love: _____
- How can you bring more of that into your life immediately? _____
- When can you make that happen? _____

Example: Design, How: Decorate room, When: Right now

- Friend
- Write down something a friend of yours loves: _____
- How can you bring more of that into their life? _____
- When can you make that happen? _____

Example: Reading, How: Offer to read a book at the same time, When: Tomorrow

- Friends
- Write down something you love doing with your friends: _____
- How can you bring more of that into your lives? _____
- When can you make that happen? _____

Example: Dinner party, How: Arrange a dinner soon, When: Next Week
- Family Member (spouse, sibling, parent, etc.)
- Write down something they love: _____
- How can you bring more of that into their life? _____
- When can you make that happen? _____

Example: Knitting, How: Ask them for a scarf and buy materials, When: This weekend
- Family
- Write down something you love doing with your friends: _____
- How can you bring more of that into your lives? _____
- When can you make that happen? _____

Example: Game Night, How: Buy new game for next time, When: This weekend
- Community
- Write down something you love doing in/with your community: _____
- How can you bring more of that into the picture? _____
- When can you make that happen? _____

Example: Bible Study, How: Talk to my church, or local church about current groups, When: Next Sunday

BONUS: Broken relationship (friend, spouse, or family)

- Write down something they used to love: _____
- How can you bring more of that into their life? _____
- When can you make that happen? _____

Example: Flowers, How: Buy/deliver little potted plant, When: Right now

Conclusion

(Next Level Leadership and Love)

Two years later, Simone moved to the States, and we got married. I stopped cheating, joined the John Maxwell Leadership Team, and started my own business. As I developed my passion, I continued to facilitate workshops and seminars: keynote speaking, emceeing weddings, and private parties. Practice becomes perfect! Implementing good leadership skills in your subconscious mind will make these skills become a part of your DNA. It becomes a natural reaction.

In chapter one, I shared that Jamaican music, culture, society, does not set up our youth for success. Men: we need to lead. This is how we can:

Limit your extended resources

I recall the shock I had when I met my two youngest brothers at my dad's funeral. I finally discovered where the additional three loaves of bread were going. The culture I was raised in promotes and supports men having multiple women and children with different women. Some men know that the women they are sleeping with are not the women they would marry. But, they insist on having a baby with these women anyways. Men intend to hold the prideful title of father at an early age. We can start leading by stop having children with multiple women. This way, all your resources would be under one household. It was embarrassing when my dad heard my name on the radio for the first time and purchased soccer shoes for me that I could not wear. All because he could not afford to buy a more quality soccer shoe because he had other kids to support financially. In some way, the child/ren loses. It is more effective and so much easier having all your children under one household. In this manner, you can lead, manage, and guide everyone within that household. Children learn from their eyes. If you are absent, your words weigh very little and sometimes can become damaging rather than developing.

Lead with love

One of the attributes of leadership is leading by example. I believe we must show our children and families how we want them to live. For those of us who are leaders, this is similar to what we do as work leaders or what we expect from others. The same applies at home. We must try the things we are asking those who follow us to do. Leadership is influencing others, and this influence can be used positively or negatively. True leadership is displaying love, which means you will try everything in your power to ensure those you lead succeed to their full potential. This should be displayed in action through physical and mental support. Have a conversation to know the person more. When you love someone, you try to meet their wants and needs. The same applies at home and at work. You must lead with love. When my behaviors became consistent at home and work, I saw tremendous success. I felt more fulfilled as a man. I strongly recommend whatever behaviors and skills we display at home should be displayed at work and vice versa. Today, all my family and close friends know I love them because every time we speak, I tell them these words before we separate. Men: let's express, share, and show love to our families, friends, and those we lead in the workplace.

Seek therapy and coaching

If you are having personal problems, I strongly recommend seeking therapy. Once the issue is identified, seek a coach to work on developing the areas identified in therapy. To this day, everyone that I have encouraged to seek therapy and coaching afterward has seen tremendous changes in their personal and professional lives. They feel fulfilled at the end of each day. Life is not balanced, but we hear the myth that we need to try and balance life. We need to prioritize, understanding each stage of our journey, so we can make the biggest impact. My brother always says, "One cannot be effective if they do not understand their reality." What he meant was that once you know exactly where you are in life, you can make the uncomfortable changes to grow and succeed. Go, seek therapy!

Find an accountability partner

In Jamaica, our culture encourages young men to hang out on the street corner and this continues today, as well as in gangs in the US. I believe the reason for this is because men were created to share, communicate, and develop through teachings. In Jamaica, men's fellowship is through communicating on the corner, but the moment they are at home, they become silent. Few words are spoken at home, and whenever there were words, they were negative. This is not setting up youth for success in life. I strongly recommend finding an accountability partner and be honest and open with them. They are similar to a therapist but more on the personal aspect. They will begin to know you and strive to see you succeed. I meet with Michael once a month, and we share, follow up on goals, and deadlines. We also talk about family. You must inspect what you expect, ask questions, conduct research, and test some things for yourself.

Develop your strength

Growing up, I was taught to identify your weaknesses and develop them. I have always thought this did not make sense but could not find an alternative. While studying John Maxwell's leadership books and attending seminars, I found the alternative. John shared once during a video session that, as leaders, we should focus on developing our strength and find others to do the work in the areas we are considered to be weak. John was not saying to be ignorant of your weakness. Others are strong in those areas, so use their strength, and build a strong foundation.

When it boils down to it, people will pay for what you are good at, your strength. So, develop those strengths and master your passion. Enhancing your strength and creating healthy relationships will allow others to help your passion come alive.

Men: let us lead with love, integrity, honesty, and trust!

Compared to leadership, love is not taught in my culture to men. As a religious island, we are not following the instruction that is given to us by God. The instruction was, *men love your wife, like how God loves the church.* From my experience, research, and study, when it comes to choosing the person we spend the rest of our lives with, we are not taught how to choose them. With all our degrees and experience, whenever someone starts a new job no matter at what level, there is some form of training. I believe we need to take the same approach with our leadership roles and as parents. Teach our children how to love.

Marlon, after years of studies with me on this journey of love for men, discovered a way one can choose the person they want to spend the rest of their lives with. Write your vision down, and I truly believe God will make it possible. In one of our many conversations, Marlon shared this process with me. One needs to create a list called *The Attributes of My Spouse.* This list will have three columns: MUST-SHOULD-COULD column.

Each column has a different meaning. You list each priority you have in a partner. This list should not be shared with anyone because it displays the attributes of your partner and takes approximately three to four months to create. As you observe yourself and the things that are a priority to you, the list will increase. It took me five months to create my list of the attributes of my wife.

Here are the meanings of each column:

1. The MUST-HAVE column is the top priority. No compromising in this area. The partner must come with these behaviors. A character that was on my MUST-HAVE column was I was seeking a partner who revered/respected or feared God. What this means was that I was not looking for a sanctified woman, but when we pray, she must understand the seriousness and attention needed to give to God. Another one on my list was finding a partner who is family oriented. I did not want to argue about not going to a family member's house or a family member coming over during holidays. These were important to me. Do not compromise in this column. If you ask, God will meet your needs.
2. The SHOULD-HAVE column is the second priority. In this area, the partner does not have to come with the behavior/character but must be open to learning it. In my SHOULD column, I had the behavior/character of seeking someone willing to learn how to cook. I can cook and wanted a partner willing to learn so that I may teach. I know that my passion has me traveling at times,

so I wanted my children to have a warm home-cooked meal. These behaviors can be shared.
3. Last but not least is the COULD-HAVE column. In this area, the partner may not come with the behavior/character. It does not matter because you will fill that area. On my list in the could column, I wanted a partner that does not need to clean on a regular basis because I clean all the time. Only in illness and due travel, my partner can step in.

These steps have helped me tremendously in choosing my second wife, Simone. With this list embedded in the subconscious area of our minds, we can eliminate the individuals we interact with and consider.

♦ ♦ ♦

The very same thing that is holding you back held me back when I was considering launching my business. That is FEAR!

The Bible says, "Don't fear, for I have redeemed you; I have called you by name; you are mine."

The word fear is used in the Bible over 80 times for a reason. God knew we would be tempted and have doubt. There are many examples in the bible for us to see how to not be fearful. I am confirming what others before have said: make moves towards your passion and dreams. Everything else will fall in place. I launched my business and tackled all my fears. Later I confirmed I was living a fulfilled life by teaching, training, coaching, and speaking. Influencing others was my purpose-driven life.

As a leader or parent, one can reduce or get rid of fear by having an accountability partner. But communication is key. The more you are informed the less fearful you will feel. Build a strong relationship with your accountability partner or those who sincerely care about you and can hold you accountable for your words and actions.

Leaders and parents, I encourage you to seek this change you desire. Change is inevitable. With no change, there is no improvement. Lead by example. Everything you know your children should know as well. Walk with them on their journey, to be a support and guide. In this manner, it is easier as a leader or parent to hold others accountable for their behavior.

Lead with love. I believe it and have seen it work. Leadership is love; love is leadership. It is all possible and worthwhile and such an amazing ride. Stick to the process!

With all those experiences, stories, processes, if you would love to move forward but need some help visit our webpage at www.emyll.org

- On our website, you can register for one of our workshops
- Purchase the study guide for the book
- Register for one-on-one coaching with me (Pete A. Kennedy)

At E.M.Y.L.L. our mission is to provide leaders, parents, schools, small and large organizations, churches, and non-profit organizations with the knowledge resources for operating and living a fulfilled life.

Thank you and farewell!

Made in the USA
Middletown, DE
01 March 2025